FLAMINGOS

CAN'T

TAP DANCE

BASED ON A TRUE STORY
by
Mollie Skilss

CHAPTER 1

The sky began to rumble as if it were a dieter's hungry stomach. It built into a roar and subsided into elevator quietness. All motion stopped. Silence. Then a thundering explosion ripped into the night.

A yellow ball glowed in the sky. The yellow turned into multi-colors. A bold blue was followed by a precious pink and a gradual green slid into a velvet violet. The color changes resembled a jawbreaker being licked by the sky.

Gleaming like perfect dental work a burst of white light illuminated the entire sky. Blobs of this white light broke off from this illumination and started to move in a fluttering motion. The few Air Force men who were present knew without question that these were angels.

There was a perfect peace on the ground as the angels filled the sky. The mandated party ceased. Everyone was entranced by the hovering angels. As they looked up at the sky, their eyes reflected an inner and outer peace. The collective calm lingered.

Wafting through the crowd was a fragrance. It was a sweet and gentle combination of carmel and vanilla. No doubt it was heaven scent.

This phenomenal event lingered so that no one could tell you how long it lasted. It was true timelessness. These people felt like they were loosely wrapped in soft blankets. It was a true comfort zone for being in the midst of a World War II prisoner of war camp.

The crowd's calm was only broken by their eyelashes blinking over and over. Their eye blinks whisked away any memory of the miracle. No one would have any recall of this moment. The bright lights fostered faster blinking.

People looked sweetly stunned. As they sat on the ground, they collectively began to hum. This hum filled the air with a glorious kind of music that Mozart would have envied.

Sleep sighed softly over all of them. None had an inkling of the majesty of the moment.

The lights disappeared. Next Air Force planes landed and loaded the sleeping bodies like the special cargo they were. Like all things military it was done with dispatch.

The flight back to The United States was smooth. Refueling caused no one to stir as the length of the trip didn't either.

The lights of Ohio's Wright Field gave them an unseen welcome. Security was tight. Lips were tighter. The relaxed passengers continued to be in a deep sleep so that unloading them out of the aircraft was a piece of cupcake.

A snap to attention cracked through the air with a salute to follow.

"Sir, how do we proceed with them now?"

The Three Star General leveled his gaze. In his lifetime he had never experienced anything as troubling or thrilling as this.

"Nothing, Colonel." The Three Star inhaled his cigarette smoke as if it were a reprieve. "THEY take over now." The General pointed his eyes in that direction.

Three men in suits were striding over to them. These crisp officials had to do the deed. The suit with a tan spoke.

"Well done, General. We will take it from here."

The General hesitated before turning to leave. Would he and the Colonel be shot in the back for being part of this? His stomach turned over like he would in his grave. No life. No more poker games. No more whiskey. No more family times. He had never turned on his heel so slowly as he took a deep breath off of his cigarette, He cupped his cigarette to make himself less of a visible target.

A hacking cough startled the General and he tripped in his anxious haste. He staggered back up to his full ramrod height. No one had seemed to see him fall and maybe it was just that no one cared that he fell. There were bigger fish to broil.

The General was alive, but not kicking. He stepped off to H.Q. where he found the Colonel had also lived not to tell.

That night the General finished three more packs of cigarettes. Even so, he was breathing easier.

Wright Air Field is an Air Force Base in Ohio. Later its name was changed to Wright-Patterson.

Ohio is a state as well as a state of being. A large part of Ohio is rural. Bumpy hills taper the landscape. Ireland may have every shade of green, but Ohio has bold splashes of primary colors. Green grass is punctuated with yellow dandelions that have gasoline colored dragon flies patrolling the whole scenery. Clover fattened bumblebees (wearing stripes because they are more slimming) float as they happily hum by cows. The cows mind their own beeswax just becud. Keeping track of what is in their four tummies occupies enough of their time.

Red Ohio barns dare the colorblind. The essence of Jonathan apples flows through the air. Colors edge up against each other as if in an Ohio State football huddle. The red apples are the legacy of Johnny Appleseed who planted many of his seeds in Ohio. His apple corps lives on with every fall apple crop.

Buckeyes are found here and there. They have a brilliant sheen. It is a shame that they are not used as a building material. If they were inlaid with buckeyes, tabletops would gleam like mahogany.

Ohio is a cheerful sounding state. It has been suggested that Ohioans have such a good sense of humor because the two O's that start and finish Ohio are begging to be made into smiley faces.

It is a good state and goodhearted as one can tell by looking at its heart shape. Ohio seems to have a steady heartbeat too.

No wonder it was a logical place to center what was about to happen. Ohio was the calm place before the storm that could be long dormant.

As he puffed his last cigarette, the General reflected. Keep things in control. Keep everybody happy. If only everyone could slip a lucky buckeye in their pocket, this could all go away except for one detail: it was too late.

The General went to look for a few cups of coffee. He also wanted to find the Lieutenants who had come back with the aircraft. The public did not know it yet, but the War with Germany was over. Angels had somehow mediated the end. The General's curiosity had reached flotilla proportions.

It took a while, but the General managed to locate the Lieutenants. They had not been debriefed yet, so the General knew they were his fair game for now. The Lieutenants were in their early twenties. Both were the same height and could have been twins if not looked at closely enough. What distinguished them from each other was that one was dark haired and the other was blond. This was no help with their hats on.

The General studied them as they stood at attention. They had a strange look in their eyes.

"At ease, men. Have a cigarette if you want."

"No, sir. I've lost all desire to smoke---ever again."

The General empathized. "So what you saw was that upsetting?"

The other Lieutenant spoke up. "It was a powerful miracle. I know this sounds crazy, but angels came out of nowhere and ended the War. Angels are the real Air Force."

The General taunted him. "So Gabriel is a pilot now?"

"We were not hallucinating, sir."

"My mistake," said the General. "You know how farfetched this sounds?"

"The way the angels mediated the end of the War is something humans couldn't have put into effect."

"What do you mean?" The General's curiosity could not hold hold off any longer. He was running out of time before the debriefing would take place.

"I don't know all the details. The suits know that better. All I know is that the angels transported Hitler and Eva Braun to the U.S. to an undisclosed location. Then there were prisoners freed from the camp we found ourselves in. Those are the passengers we brought back. They look sedated, but they are under angel power. There are some notable people among those passengers."

"Who?" asked the General. His curiosity was beyond containment at this point.

The Lieutenant half smiled. "All I can say with the angels and all that divine intervention is 'God knows.'"

At that moment the General wished he had two more stars.

****

The three suits were gathered in the room where the transported passengers were laying around like lost luggage. The three suits laughed without concern that they would wake anyone up.

"Did you see the look on that General's face?" said the suit with a tan. "His medals reflected the terror in his face."

"What does he exactly know?" asked the skinny suit.

"What he knows and what he believes are two different things. He was told that the cargo was precious stuff from angels," said the suit in charge.

"Like haloes," joked the suit with a tan.

The suit in charge glared. "This is way too serious to take things so lightly. The angels ended this awful war and now we have to tie up the loose ends. We need to be grateful instead of being clowns."

The skinny suit showed some authenticity. "I'm uncomfortable with angels showing up to fight our battles for us. Has this ever happened before?"

The suit in charge looked at him with appreciation for his question. "Yes. It was in either 1250 A.D. or in 1500 A.D. where there was a battle going on in Mongolia. From what I understand it was on horseback. One side was losing very badly. It was a massacre. Suddenly the sky opened up to massive light. The light or the angels took over and defeated the side that had been winning."

The three suits quieted. The suit with a tan ventured to make a comment. "So this has been some kind of holy war we've been waging?"

The suit in charge finally smiled. "Yes, it has been on a wing and a prayer."

The skinny suit scanned the place they were in. It looked like a domed, metallic building that was the length of a football field. It was actually an airplane hangar. There were no airplanes in it. The only occupants were the three suits and the twenty-five passengers who had just been transported back.

The suit in charge noticed the skinny suit's observation. "Yes, we have our work cut out for us. Time to loosen our ties, take off our jackets, and roll up our sleeves."

The suit with a tan spoke up. "What are we supposed to be doing?"

"Let me explain," said the suit in charge. "The angels appeared to a high ranking military officer on our side and conveyed the plan. The angels found Hitler and his mistress Eva Braun and brought them back to the Americans. They freed the German's prisoners-of-war. Those prisoners are the twenty-five we have here. A handful are very notable."

The suit in charge paused. "For unknown reasons the angels want the notable people to have disguised identities and have whole new lives."

The skinny suit reacted. "I'm not one to question the burning bush."

The suit with a tan shot back his response. "Never beat a dead rose bush."

The suit in charge got back in control. "O.K., guys. This is what we are going to do. We are going to try and identify each person. According to the angels there will be clues on each person and we will have more than adequate time to do this. Then we have to separate out the notables. We are in charge of giving each notable a new identity to give each of them a new life."

The skinny suit looked pensive. "I don't know if it's my divine right to interfere with other people's lives like this."

The suit with a tan looked like he had given away his sense of humor. "Yeah, and how do angels communicate with us anyway?"

The suit in charge looked at both of them as if they had fallen off of Pluto. "Are you two telling me you don't want to do this because you are afraid?"

The suit with a tan had tried to pass it off as a joke, but he knew this task troubled him. It reminded him of his swimming hole as a kid. The only way to get into the water was to jump off a high cliff. It didn't help that it was called Dead Man's Leap. He always had a warm feeling of terror wash over him before he made the jump.

"I guess this is some kind of leap of faith," he said.

"Exactly," said the suit in charge. "We were picked for a reason. One of those reasons is that we can keep our mouthes shut. Another reason is that we can get this job done with creativity and compassion. In the Bible the angels say, 'Fear not.' There's not going to be any type of retribution here."

The skinny suit persisted. This was a good question. "How do angels communicate with us?"

"Whenever and however they want," said the suit in charge. Then his eyes twinkled. "I understand it has something to do with harps and trumpets." That ended the discussion and that was why he was the suit in charge.

The suit with a tan got back to the business at hand. He was ready to take his leap. "What are we supposed to do with these people? Will they ever wake up?"

The suit in charge was glad that some of the tension had diffused. He was secretly pleased with his harp and trumpet answer. "Lord, make me an instrument of thy peace," he said to himself.

The suit in charge began giving directions. He had been the oldest child in his family and was quite skilled at bossing others around. One day he made the mistake of bossing his mother around and found that there were limits to his authority. His mother was fixing him an egg for breakfast. Bellowing at her like he was giving an order he demanded, "DON'T PUT PEPPER ON MINE!"

She brought over his plate, smiled sweetly, and said, "Be careful how you treat people because you'll never know what you'll get back."

His mother set his plate in front of him and an egg swimming in a black layer of pepper stared back at him. He got a distaste of his own medicine that day and learned the lesson about respect.

Now he had become an effective leader and one who did not force his will. He began to guide the other two suits. "Don't worry that they will come out of their slumber. Check for any identification around the wrist or neck. Search pockets. Dog tags will certainly be helpful. We have twenty-five folks here to identify. Twenty-one of them will be reunited with their loved ones. Four will start new lives that we create for them."

The suit with a tan decided to plunge into the task. He looked in the pockets of a man who was snoozing comfortably. The suit with a tan was afraid he would wake up the guy. The guy's pockets were a treasure trove. The best thing was a photo of someone the suit with a tan imagined was the guy's wife. She resembled Carole Lombard. Then the suit with a tan found something startling. It was a piece of paper with hand lettered words that said, "Fear not!" The piece of paper and photo were stuffed back into the guy's pocket. The guy's neck was checked next. Dog tags hung down ready to be read. His identity was secured. Here was Jasper Stevens from Stockton, California.

The suit in charge came over. "Good work. Let's put him in the next room where he will be transported to the infirmary until he wakes up."

The suits worked for the next sixty minutes and had searched seventeen people. Clues as to identities were blatant and some were subtle. One man's wedding ring had an inscription inside which included his name. A key ring with the name of a local bowling alley put together with his name on the wedding ring would make it relatively easy to place him back where he belonged.

Of the eight people left, two were women out of a group that was predominately men. No notables had been found yet. They were getting close.

They stopped in front of a slumbering G.I. as they could tell by his uniform. He was good looking in every sense of the word. The suit in charge almost hated to disrupt his anonymity.

The soldier's uniform was dingy and dirt betrayed the fact that he had seen some rough times. His full head of hair showed that it had been some time since he had gotten a military cut.

The soldier's dog tags dangled an invitation to look. The suit grabbed them. After spending a full minute pondering them, the suit in charge gave a low whistle. "Unbelievable."

The skinny suit wanted to know what was so impossible. "Who is it?"

The suit with a tan waited for the announcement. Starting today he knew anything was possible.

The suit in charge shared the soldier's identity. "He's Joseph P. Kennedy Jr."

The suit with a tan spoke first. "The pilot? I thought he went down with his plane."

The suit in charge searched his memory like he had been searching these slumbering people. "If I remember correctly, there was some disagreement about what happened. No body was ever found. There was even a report that he had been captured by the enemy."

The skinny suit made his observation. "He looks really good after you imagine the stress he has gone through."

The suit in charge remembered something else. "Too bad his eyes are closed. The Kennedys are supposed to have the most intense blue eyes that there are. They are as bright as the ocean when it sparkles on a sunny day."

The trio of suits moved on. This time they paused in front of a beautiful woman. The suits were unable to figure out how to identify her. The woman had a jeweled locket around her neck. Being men they overlooked the significance of the locket initially. They tried to find engraving on the back of it, but the gold was as smooth as her skin.

The suit with a tan had a flash of insight which he wondered later whether it came from an angel. "This isn't any old necklace," he said. "It's a locket."

None of them had fingernails so it took a few moments to force it open. Inside was a small photo.

"Who is it?" asked the skinny suit.

"Now I know," said the suit in charge. "The picture is Rose Kennedy. I recognize her daughter here. She's Kathleen Kennedy otherwise known as Kik."

"Didn't she go down in a plane crash over Europe too?"

"Yes. I can't explain it." The suit in charge looked puzzled. "Let's keep going. I wasn't sure what kind of surprises we were going to run across."

The suits identified more people and were down to the last two. A man was snoring so that it sounded like he was emitting bubbles. His hair was unruly black and his eye color was undetermined. He looked to be about 18 and he was not in uniform. There were no dog tags.

"Do you think this is another Kennedy?" asked the suit with a tan.

The suit in charge reached into the guy's pants pocket. Pulling out a full sheet of paper that had been handled extensively, he noticed it was written in German. There were some kind of official notarizations on it. "Either one of you read German?"

The skinny suit took the official looking document. He eyed it carefully like it might explode. It was an emotional bombshell all right. "I don't know how this can be possible."

"What is it?" said the suit in charge.

"The man's name is Gustav. This document permits him to travel anywhere in Germany that he wants as well as in any countries occupied by Germany."

"Why is that?" asked the suit in charge.

"Because." There was a pregnant with quintuplets pause before he answered. "He is Hitler's son."

"No," said the suit with a tan. "Hitler did not have any children. It was even rumored that he was gay!"

"Hitler may have wanted to protect his children. Anyway, it's not ours to question."

The suit with a tan persisted. "What were those angels thinking?"

The suit in charge wanted to distract from the issue. "Let's move on and see who we have here."

The last mystery surprise was a woman with close cropped wavy hair. She appeared older than the other three. She had crows feet from a presumable sense of humor or maybe from squinting into the sun. What really stood out was her aviator jacket.

The three suits gawked. They all recognized her.

Amelia Earhart had been found.

CHAPTER 2

The future is hidden even from the men who make it...Anatole France

The three suits were in a conference room. They had discovered the hidden treasures. Now it was time to hide them again.

The suit in charge outlined their mission. "Now is our chance to be creative. We must reinvent these people. Give them new identities and new lives. It's what is officially called reconfiguring. They will never recall anything about their lives up to the point where they are reconfigured."

The skinny suit was curious. "How is that done?"

"I'll show you the lab. Follow me," said the suit in charge.

They went down two long hallways and down a flight of steps. There was a door at the bottom of the steps that had three padlocks on it. The suit in charge unlocked them deftly without bumbling any of the three different keys.

The door swung open and another door faced them. This one had a combination lock. The suit in charge twirled it easier than a pencil.

This door took some heft to push it to enter the room. The room was dark like misty twilight. It took the suits a moment for their eyes to adjust. A pleasant mint scent hung around them.

It was comfortably cool. There were recliner type chairs scattered around. Rows and rows of glass bottles lined the room. They contained brightly colored liquids. A few refrigerators were jammed into a corner. An operating table was off to the side.

The suit with a tan wasn't sure what he was seeing. "What do they do with this stuff?"

"They take the new biographies and hypnotize these people. They reprogram them with every detail we have provided. Food is given as a conditioning tool. You know, positive reinforcement. The colored liquids are given because they seal in their repressed past so they don't remember it again. It's done intravenously."

The skinny suit wondered out loud about the operating table.

"That's not totally up to us," said the suit in charge. "The reconfigurers have to use their discretion about altering someone's appearance."

The suit with a tan had a more disturbing question as far as he was concerned. "Is this what will happen to us once we finish our assignment here?"

"We have orders not to disclose what we've done here. Then we should be o.k."

"The President's orders?"

The suit in charge was direct. "No, the angels."

There was that leap again.

They returned to the conference room. It was time to put lives back together.

"Who should we start with?" asked the suit in charge.

Neither suit offered an opinion. The suit in charge liked that he had to make a decision. "We will start with Kathleen Kennedy. What name should we give her?"

More silence ensued. The suit in charge had to break this stalemate.

"We are brainstorming here. You are giving these people an opportunity of a new life. They may have been notable people in the past, but now they might enjoy the comfort of anonymity. We can provide them with personality and qualities that they have always wanted. After we are done with them, they will have free will. Let's prepare them well."

The suit with a tan volunteered a name. "How about Helen after Helen of Troy? It shows that she is a strong woman."

"Helen it is," said the suit in charge. "I know you guys are creative so let's go at it."

"Let's put her in college. There's a small Ohio college near here where she can live on campus. It's called Asgood College." The skinny suit was warming up to the task.

"Her major can be Drama." The suit with a tan thought Helen would enjoy that.

The skinny suit brought up a concern. "Can we request no plastic surgery on her? She's so beautiful."

The suit in charge considered this. "That is a point well taken. Why take away that gift? What we might have to do to throw people off is to get rid of her Boston accent. The Kennedys have that distinct accent. We will have to give her a Midwest sound."

"Favorite game?"

"Chinese checkers."

"No, we need something more complex."

"O.K. How about bridge and she hates Monopoly?"

"Sounds good."

"Favorite perfume?"

"Definitely Chanel No. 5."

"Favorite food?"

"Prime rib."

"Sounds like a good idea for right now."

The suits laughed, but they were tired and hungry.

"Favorite drink?"

"Nondrinker, but she enjoys her coffee."

"Cream and sugar or black?"

"In a cup or a mug?"

"Hold on." The suit with a tan was bothered. "Let this be up to her."

The suit in charge could see his point. "Let's move on."

"Religion?"

"Let's have her try being Protestant. She will be very devout."

"Political party?"

"In the interest of her new identity she should be Republican."

"Favorite music?"

"Definitely Glenn Miller with 'In the Mood' as her favorite song."

"So she likes to jitterbug."

"She is a lot of fun and has a distinct laugh."

"Her best quality?"

"Honesty."

"That's ironic."

"What she knows as her personal honesty."

The suits continued and put her personal history together. Her parents were deceased. She was at Asgood College on a scholarship. Helen grew up on an Ohio farm. The suits added every possible detail to her traits and background. Then they had her taken to the reconfiguring lab that they had seen earlier.

Next was Joe Kennedy Jr.

The brainstorming had picked up its pace.

"His accent has to go too. Make it Midwest."

"No Southern drawl?"

That comment was ignored.

"Let's do some surgery on his nose. It has to be made bigger."

"He will favor long crew cuts."

"He served in the Navy."

"His Navy tattoo we give him will be proof of that. He loves to sail."

"Chain smoker."

"Martini man."

"Shaken or stirred?"

"Free will," a suit insisted.

"Graduate of The University of Chicago."

"Lives in Chicago where he grew up."

"Has a tremendous sense of humor. His laugh is a blend of a hacking cigarette cough and a guffaw."

"Diehard Republican."

"Agnostic."

"Favorite food is beef stroganoff."

"Black coffee drinker?"

"No choice for him?"

"He needs black coffee for his hangovers."

"Likes to read. Makes sure he reads the newspaper every morning."

"Very kind underneath."

"Generous."

"Likes word games."

"Father abandoned the family when he was a youngster. Has a mother who is living."

The suits put the finishing touches on Joe's story. They filled in more depth about his personality, beliefs and values. Then they realized they had not given him a name.

"I like John," said the skinny suit. "It will be in honor of his real brother."

"Last name?"

"Jones?" The suit with a tan did not like his own suggestion at all.

The suit in charge recognized that. "Here's a whole pool of names." He pulled out a telephone directory. "I am going to point and pick."

He opened the book and slammed his finger onto a page. "His name is now officially John Kendricks."

Looking around at the other suits he asked, "Anything more you can think of?"

The other suits shook their heads.

Amelia Earhart was next. The suits gathered around her in disbelief and awe. She looked so relaxed and content that it seemed like a shame to disrupt her life. Maybe she wanted it disrupted. Who knew what she had been subjected to for all these years where she had been missing? Maybe she did not want to be such a high flying profile person.

"Why don't we start with her name?"

"It should be something unique and very feminine."

The suit in charge took this one over. "She will be Estrella Kendricks."

"Kendricks like in John Kendricks?"

The suit in charge was not going to waver on this one. The coffee and martini issues could be moot points, but this was too important. "There's an eighteen year age gap between Estrella and John. She is going to be his mother."

The other suits knew this was definite by the suit in charge's tone. The suit in charge realized how he had sounded. The taste of pepper suddenly flooded his memory and his saliva became acrid. He decided to back off and have the other suits take more of a role like they had been.

"Estrella is perfect as long as we don't make her favorite game be poker," said the skinny suit.

"No, it's mahjong," said the suit with a tan. They were off and running.

"What does she do for a living?"

"Breathe."

They laughed and the suit in charge no longer had the taste of pepper to contend with in his mouth.

"Let's make her a kindergarten teacher."

"Hobbies?"

"She loves to cook. Even so, her favorite food is ice cream."

"Any speciality?"

"She makes a dessert with freshly sliced peaches topped with brown sugar and a dollop of sour cream."

"Any other things that she likes? After all, she really is Amelia Earhart and we need to give her a life that is a little bit more exciting than cottage cheese."

They pondered this for a while. The suit in charge volunteered an idea that was not barked like an order given to the cook in a diner. "Why don't we have her take one flying lesson a month?"

"Yeah, and her instructor won't be able to get over what a natural she is."

The suits laughed together again. They were pleased with themselves. They were happy to bring some pleasure into Amelia's new life like they had added Joe's love of sailing to his new life.

"Let's take a break, men. Estrella and John have to go down to the Reconfiguring Room."

Sandwiches and Cokes® materialized for the suits. As they ate, the suit with a tan realized he was actually more tired and in need of sleep than he was hungry. He was thankful for the food though. They ate in silence since they had been talking nonstop for hours to create new identities for their new charges. It was a strange responsibility, but each suit felt honored to have been selected to do the task. The skinny suit wondered how he had come to the attention of an angel to be picked for this. The suit with a tan was more paranoid. He worried that angels might be keeping too close tabs on him. The suit in charge just wished that the angels had supplied some chocolate cake or at least angel food cake for their meal.

Their last task lay fast asleep in front of the suits.

"It makes you think about what all he has been through," said the skinny suit.

"Or what a privileged life he has led," said the suit with a tan.

"Men, we need to look forward, not backwards," said the suit in charge. "We are all about the future."

"O.K. We know the drill," said the skinny suit.

"Wait." The suit with a tan was clearly bothered. "We need to be very careful. This is Hitler's son. One thing we have to make sure is that he never holds any prejudices."

"Good thinking," said the suit in charge. They were off to a good start.

"Name?"

"Bud."

"Last name?"

"Telephone book time."

The suit with a tan opened the book and placed his finger. Little did he know he had nothing to do with the selection, but it was divine intervention. "His new name is Skilss."

"What does he like to do?"

"He's very athletic and a great basketball player. He loves all kinds of sports and can't get enough of listening to games on the radio." The skinny suit liked bestowing this trait.

"Background?"

"He's a farm boy," said the suit in charge. "He's going to be reunited with his parents on a rundown farm in Ohio. His parents are Hitler and Eva as you know and they are being reconfigured by some others. Bud has a basketball scholarship to Asgood College where Helen Troyer is also a student. The administration of that college is cooperating with us. Of course they don't know the truth, but are allowing sudden enrollment of our two students."

"Let's make Bud very hard working with a tremendous sense of humor. He knows how to tell a story."

I think it's important to make him a nondrinker."

"He's also a dog lover."

"He loves the newspaper comics."

They worked on more details of his personal history and personality. They were pleased with all that they had done.

Suddenly they became very sleepy. Unbeknownst to them their Cokes® had been laced with something that would erase their memory of this particular night and what they had done. Someone came and put them in their cars.

One suit was driven to a grocery store parking lot and left. One suit was driven to a high school parking lot and left. The last suit was left in a church parking lot.

Waking up in a strange parking lot remained a mystery for all three suits for the rest of their lives. They also wondered why they avoided drinking Cokes® from then on. Another inexplicable thing they had in common was an aversion to the saying, "No good deed goes unpunished."

CHAPTER 3

Helen woke up to the sound of birds chirping. She felt well rested as if she had slept for days. Little did she know that she had and even more.

She stayed in bed a little longer to enjoy the feeling. It was like waiting to leave a movie theater until she had read every credit. A tune was skipping through her head. She smiled as she recognized "In the Mood."

Scanning the room Helen saw the outfit she had apparently laid out for herself to wear on this first day of college. There was a vase with Queen Anne's Lace on her desk. The only wall decor was a movie poster of Humphrey Bogart. She winked at him from her bed. Maybe she would star in a movie with him someday.

She had somehow awakened before the alarm clock had gone off. Alarm clocks were a rude awakening to the day as far as Helen was concerned. They were a shrill nag.

Helen slid her feet to the wood floor. Upon sitting up she felt a bit woozy, but chalked it up to the anticipation of the day. She reached for the radio knob and big band music filled the room and her soul. Helen did a dance step over to her clothes. She got dressed and carefully did her hair which she considered her best feature. Others would argue that her blue eyes were her best feature. By no means was Helen vain, but she did like to present herself in the best possible light. She really did not have to do anything special for others to take notice of her.

Next she had to get to the dining hall. She craved some bacon and eggs and especially some coffee. Suddenly she felt conflicted. Did she want her coffee black or with cream and sugar or with just cream? She wondered how something so simple could cause her such consternation?

She decided to think about other things. Who might she meet today that would become a friend? Would she have to get on stage today to act in her Drama class? Would she understand what in the world what was being taught in Algebra?

Having reached the dining hall Helen Troyer had made her decision. She would have her coffee with cream.

Bud Skilss woke up in his dorm room He had a splitting headache. Looking around his room he tried to get his bearings. He felt like a ship coming through the fog. The bright light streaming through the window punctuated his headache. This was not a good start to his first day of college. Bud lay in bed and tried to motivate himself to get going. The first thing he tried was to hold his pillow over his face and hum as loudly as he could. That felt a little better.

Then he thought of all the things he was grateful for in his life. He struggled with this and felt frustrated that this wasn't easier. For some reason he was drawing blanks.

He rubbed his temples with his fingers. Slowly he climbed out of bed and ran cold water over his face. Then he shaved and took deep breaths.

By now he felt a little better. He gathered his books and finally remembered he had basketball practice later in the afternoon. Meanwhile, his first priority was to get over to the dining hall for some black coffee. The thought of introducing anything else to his stomach was out of the question. Bud wondered why he felt so bad. He consoled himself by believing it would be a temporary state of being.

He arrived at the dining hall and the breakfast smells swirling about were enough to turn his stomach further. He spotted the big coffee urn in the corner and began a quick path over to it. Unfortunately, as he did so, he bumped into a woman carrying a cup of coffee. The coffee spilled over her and managed to miss Bud.

Bud was quick to apologize. First, he noticed how her dress was drenched with a brown color and then his eyes fell on her beauty.

Helen's poise was automatic. "I knew that brown was the color to wear today."

"You didn't get burned did you?" Bud was concerned.

"Oh, you haven't had your coffee this morning. It's just lukewarm."

Bud's head was about to slice in two. He did manage to introduce himself. "I'm Bud Skilss. Let me buy you a cup of coffee some time."

Bud noticed that when he spoke there was a gutteral sound that wanted to erupt from his throat.

Helen laughed. Bud thought she sounded like wind chimes.

She made a light joke. "I guess this cup was on me." She noticed that her voice had a nasal sound. Maybe it was an allergy.

Helen moved on and Bud sat by himself at another table. He noticed that she was sitting with three other women. It was like looking at a diamond surrounded by chipmunks.

Bud had not realized how hungry he was. With exuberance born of being famished he tore into his breakfast of bacon and eggs. Suddenly a guy sat next to him.

"Where did you learn to wield your silverware like that? You're supposed to set down the fork and transfer it to your other hand. You look like a dang German otherwise."

Voltage coursed through Bud's body. It was a sensation he had never remembered feeling before. Then he felt faint. He blinked a couple of times and gulped at his coffee. Just like that his headache was gone.

"My name is Bud."

"I'm Buck. Just trying to help."

"Would you show me what you mean with the fork? This is how we do it on the farm."

Buck was happy to be a tine tutor. Bud was a quick study.

"You are tall," said Buck. "We could use you on the basketball team."

"I may not know how to use a fork, but I can shoot baskets," said Bud. "I'm here on a full basketball scholarship."

"Double dang," said Buck. "I play guard."

"I will see you later in the gym," said Bud. Then he finished his eggs as he fumbled with his fork.

Helen was upset with the brown stain on her dress. She went back to her room and washed it out as best she could. She did not have much money to buy new clothes. That Bud was certainly clumsy.

She looked in the mirror and was thankful to catch the piece of egg at the corner of her mouth. Her eyes caught her eye. Until that moment she had not realized how striking they were. Maybe her hair wasn't her best physical attribute.

It was time for class. She had that mix of excitement and dread. That was especially so for her first class which was Algebra. Math wasn't meant to be a factor in her life as far as she was concerned. Knowing how to balance a checkbook was enough to get through life successfully.

Helen picked up her math book and realized she only had two minutes to get to class. Punctuality was not one of her best qualities.

The first thing Bud noticed about Helen as she rushed into the classroom was that she had changed her dress. His admiration for her was eclipsed by his guilt. There was background noise that he was aware of and finally he heard his name. The professor was taking attendance.

Helen saw the stain maker. Then she turned her full attention on what the professor was teaching. He was introducing material on equations. Helen wondered how long it would be until her Drama class.

Buck was also in the class. He approached Helen when the lecture was over.

"You looked puzzled in there. I can help you if you need any help with your homework," said Buck. He could not get over her sparkling blue eyes.

"I don't know how you fit into the equation yet," laughed Helen. "If I get stuck, I will let you know."

Bud heard the wind chime laugh and saw the move that Buck had made. He had to have a date with Helen.

The next morning Bud was ready. He spotted Helen as soon as she entered the dining hall. He approached her with a cup of steaming coffee with cream.

"I thought you would like this in a cup instead of on your dress," he said.

With a smile Helen took it from him. "I like it better this way."

Bud just plunged in without thinking too much about what he was doing. It made it easier that way. "Would you like to go out with me Saturday night for a hamburger and a shake?" Bud braced himself for the answer.

Helen looked straight into his brown eyes. "That sounds like fun."

"I will pick you up at six. You don't mind walking, do you?"

"No, I've been practicing all week on campus."

"See you then and also in math class."

"It's all adding up." The wind chimes sounded off.

This time Bud smiled as he moved away and practiced with his fork again.

Later in the day Bud had basketball practice. His moves to the basket were flawless that afternoon. He glided across the court as if the floor were waxed with furniture polish. He hit every basket he shot. The other players and the coach stopped everything and watched this spectacle. Could this guy really be on their team?

Bud's secret to his performance was that he was not thinking at all about what he was doing. Instead, he was holding a picture of Helen in his head and imagining her wind chime laugh. This lent to his incredible success in shooting baskets. He felt absolutely joyful out there with his skills. This was the happiest he had been in a long time.

Practice was over too soon as far as Bud was concerned. Now he had to face his math homework. He went to the dining hall first.

Bud smiled to himself. He was glad he was not as coordinated as he was today when he bumped into Helen at breakfast. Otherwise, he would never have met her.

Buck came up to Bud to ruin the moment. "Do you think you need help in using your spoon?"

Bud countered. "Do you need help with your free throws?"

Buck backed off. "See you at square one in math class."

Three math assignments later and it was Saturday. Helen was getting ready for her date with Bud. She decided to wear the dress that Bud had spilled coffee all over. The stain had washed out well and there were no grounds to hold anything against him for his clumsiness. Singing as she brushed her hair Helen was aware how much she was looking forward to this evening with Bud.

Bud combed his unruly black hair, but could not seem to calm it down. Maybe his nerves were being transmitted through his hair follicles. He checked his sweater vest and found no stains. Using his fork the new way made it conducive to dropping bits of egg on his clothes. He whistled a tune as he made one last inspection of himself.

The air was crisp as he walked over to Helen's room. Fall was in the air. The smell of wood smoke proved it. Bud reached into his pocket and felt the only money he had left. Fortunately he was starting a janitor job at the college the next week. He was as poor as a chapel mouse.

Bud took a deep breath before he knocked on Helen's door. He exhaled and said a quick prayer.

Helen did not answer immediately. She was a believer in letting anticipation build so that the momentum created a special energy for the date.

Bud had turned away to leave when Helen opened the door. "I'll be with you in a minute." She shut the door to let the momentum crest again.

Helen came out of the door and smiled at Bud. He had been so busy being enamored with her wind chime laugh that he had not noticed her knockout smile before this. It was going to be a very nice evening. At least it would be if he didn't spill his milkshake all over her.

"Have you ever been to The Hut?"

Helen said she hadn't.

"Their speciality is hamburgers and shakes. It's very casual."

They talked easily as they made the trek to The Hut. Once they got there, they were faced with the popularity of the place. It was packed.

A booth became available and they slid in opposite of each other. The sizzling smoke of burgers being fried had seized the air. The shake machine whirred away with its captive ice cream. It was an atmosphere ready for couples like Helen and Bud.

They ordered burgers and Helen asked for a chocolate shake while Bud ordered a strawberry one. They decided to split an order of fries which Bud was thankful for because that meant he had just enough left for the tip.

Helen asked Bud where he was from.

"I grew up on a farm about twenty minutes from here. And you?"

"I grew up on a farm too! It was about half an hour from here. My childhood is kind of hazy. I do remember reading to the pigs."

"The cows didn't feel slighted?" Bud decided to try another joke. "Talking about pigs reminds me of a joke."

"Oh?"

"A traveling salesman's car broke down in front of a farmer's house. He walked up to the front door and before he knocked this pig with a wooden leg ran by him. The salesman knocked on the door and the farmer answered. He asked the farmer if he could use his phone to get help. Then the salesman asked the farmer about the pig he saw.

'Oh,' said the farmer. 'One of my kids was drowning in the swimming hole one day and that pig saved his life. Another time the barn was on fire and that pig came and got me. I got trapped under my tractor another time and that pig pulled me from underneath. He saved my life.'

The salesman was intrigued. 'How did he get that wooden leg?'

'With a fine pig like that we only eat a little bit of him at a time.'"

The wind chimes tingled a melody. Bud knew he was in love.

Helen tried her hand at pig humor. "You know what they say. 'Never try to teach a pig how to sing. It wastes your time and annoys the pig.'"

Bud kept on with the theme. "I suppose you are fluent in Pig Latin."

"Oinkvay-oinkvay."

"You have a ways to go to become a translator."

They laughed and sipped their milkshakes. The reconfigurers had done a thorough job.

For the next year Helen and Bud dated exclusively. Buck tried to make a move on Helen early on, but she would have nothing to do with him. Bud and Helen went to the movies. They were partial to Westerns. They went on picnics, went to church every Sunday, and went to The Hut. Helen rooted for Bud at all of his basketball games where he mentally dedicated every rebound to Helen's honor.

Bud worked hard. Besides being a full time student he worked two part-time jobs.

After a year of dating Bud and Helen were having malts at The Hut. Bud brought up something that was difficult to do. "Helen, I would like you to meet my folks. How is next Saturday for you?"

"I would like that," she said. She knew that Bud barely talked about his parents.

"Mom said she would make dinner for us. You have to realize we live on a rundown farm, so don't expect much."

"Appearances don't mean much to me," said Helen. "I'm sure your parents are good people."

Bud was not reassured. He was not ashamed of his parents, but they had struggled all of their lives and the wear and tear had taken its toll on them. He was the first one in his family and extended family to attend college. They were proud of him, but he was sure that they thought he had changed. He was not better than anyone else, but more self conscious of his roots.

Bud and Helen arrived at the farm about eleven that Saturday morning. The farm gave ramshackle its definition. Except for the barn all the other buildings were gray. The paint had worn off ages ago. Perhaps they had never been painted. The barn's red color had faded into pink. Gaps showed through the sides of the barn. The outhouse had its half moon identification mark on its door.

Roosters and chickens strutted their stuff in the barnyard. Helen could hear the cows mooing like altos in the barn. She did not see any pigs or sheep. Flies were swarming everywhere. There was a neat, tiny garden to the side of the farm house. The paint on the farmhouse was cracked and chipped. This was a farm that was barely subsisting.

A couple of Adirondack chairs sat in the yard. They looked like they had hosted quite a few bib overalls. Bud and Helen passed by them and went to the side porch. A fly swatter hung from a nail. The screen door was also a fly deterrent. Bud knocked on it.

"Mom; Pops, we're here."

Bud's mom came to the door. She did not look happy. Her lips formed a frown. At first Helen took it personally, but later realized this was her permanent expression. She was wearing a plain flowered housedress with an apron over it. This was Emma Skilss's a.k.a. Eva Braun's new life.

In a flat voice she called, "Elmer, Bud is here."

Elmer Skilss a.k.a. Hitler lumbered into the room. He was carrying some extra pounds, but his thinning black hair was not contributing to his weight. His mustache was half gray. What struck Helen was how opposite he was to Emma. He greeted Helen ebulliently. Elmer's mood was lighthearted. It was like he didn't know there was such a thing as indoor plumbing.

Helen accompanied Emma into the kitchen where it was hot. The iron cookstove had already baked two apple pies that morning. A pump was on the counter by the sink to provide water. Emma gave Helen a bowl of potatoes. Helen began peeling them. Helen tried to make small talk. Emma was not responsive to conversation. She seemed to be singularly focused on getting Saturday dinner fixed and over with so that she could get on with her other chores.

When Helen asked her what Bud was like as a little boy, Emma stopped what she was doing. Her eyes had a combined look of vacancy and sadness as she looked into Helen's contrasting eyes.

"I couldn't tell you. I was so busy trying to get by. Those details escape me now."

Helen felt sorry for her and for Bud too. This woman was clearly depressed and poverty had been unbecoming to her mood. Helen decided to change her approach.

She carried on a monologue about how wonderful Bud was to her and some of the things they liked to do together. Helen made sure she complimented Bud's mother as much as she could. She admired the pies and talked about how much she liked mashed potatoes which they were having. Helen said she liked Emma's apron. Emma allowed that she had made it herself out of a feed sack.

The chicken that was being fixed was fresh. Emma had slaughtered it a few hours earlier. Helen wanted to ask what had been done with the feathers, but decided that was too forward to ask at a first meeting.

They sat down to a delicious chicken dinner. The chicken was pan fried, the green beans from the garden were cooked perfectly, the mashed potatoes and gravy couldn't have been better, and the pies completed the taste treat.

What the meal held in quality, it lacked in conversation. Elmer silently shoveled in mouthfuls of food and Emma stared at her plate as she picked at her dinner. Bud ended up supplying a monologue about Helen and also threw in some lip service about his basketball.

Finally Bud lapsed into silence. Then his eyes perked up as he looked at Helen. "Would you like to see our cow with the wooden leg?"

CHAPTER 4

The following summer Helen was hired for a job she had dreamed of for several months. She was given the position of a reporter at Wright Air Field. She could not have been more thrilled if she had gone barnstorming in a bi-plane.

Prior to leaving for the summer Bud had taken Helen to The Hut. At the bottom of her milkshake glass was a diamond ring. They were officially engaged. Both were in hog heaven.

Bud had a job in Cleveland for the summer so they would have a period of separation. On day two of their jobs they missed each other more than love letters could compensate.

Helen worked for a Three Star General who was mellow from age and from seeing so much war. When he met Helen, he squinted as he took one puff from his smoke. "You look familiar." He couldn't place her, but he was sure he had seen her before. "Cigarette?"

"No, thank you. I understand that I report to you."

"Yes," said the Three Star. "You are to meet the incoming planes and interview anyone who is interesting to you. Your stories will be published in the base newspaper. That hole in the wall over there is your office."

Helen looked over to where the Three Star had jerked his head. There was a metal desk with a typewriter on it. A pencil holder and a fan completed the desk's surface.

"Your other duty is to make sure I don't run out of cigarettes and matches. Do I make myself clear?"

"What about making coffee?"

"That's assumed. I will arrange a tour for you and then you can expect a plane to come in at thirteen hundred."

Helen performed her duties better than was expected of a civilian. Every week she cut out her articles and mailed them to Bud. He wrote back with high praise and a countdown of the days until they would see each other again.

A month after Helen started at Wright, a visitor came to see the Three Star General. The General and the visitor visited and smoked cigars. They emerged from the office and surveyed the tarmac. Helen was at some distance away conversing with a pilot.

The visitor saw Helen and was intrigued immediately. He had not seen many women here. "Who is that?" he asked.

"That's Helen Troyer, our base reporter. Would you like to meet her?"

"You know I would."

Helen turned and saw the Three Star with another man. The Three Star General gestured for her to come over.

"Helen, I have someone I would like you to meet. This is John F. Kennedy."

"You may call me Jack."

Kennedy was startled by the sight of Helen. "Will you join me at the Officers Club for a cup of coffee?" Kennedy was thinking he might need something stronger.

Helen looked at the Three Star. "Go ahead," he said.

She liked that order.

Helen knew that Kennedy was a war hero and from a prominent family. She was flattered to have a cup of coffee with him. He was so good looking that she didn't want to blink and waste any sight of him. It was eerie how his eyes resembled hers.

At the Officers Club Kennedy seated Helen at a table in the corner. They were most striking together.

Kennedy could not take his eyes off of Helen. Their coffee arrived. Finally Kennedy said what was on his mind. "You could be the identical twin of my sister Kathleen. We used to call her Kik."

"I have an all purpose face," said Helen.

"It's just uncanny. You are just like her except you don't have a Boston accent."

They connected like old friends. Helen's wind chime laugh got a work out in response to Jack's wit. Jack could not get over her charm and, of course, her looks. He remembered Justice Oliver Holme's remark about Roosevelt having "a second rate intellect and a first rate temperament." He told Helen that and said she had a "first rate everything."

She insisted that he tell her about the PT 109 rescue. At first he was reluctant, but because her interest was so genuine he told his story. It was one he rarely related.

"It is a privilege to meet a hero."

Kennedy countered. "Every soldier on this base is a hero. What was it that Will Rogers said? 'We can't all be heroes because someone has to sit on the curb and clap as they go by.'"

Jack and Helen went through three cups of coffee together. "You certainly would be a natural fit with my relatives," Jack said. "You know what they say. Heredity runs in our family."

"I had a good time," said Helen. "I wish you the best."

"For my sake it's too bad you are engaged. If you are ever at The Cape, stop by. It's a wonderful place for a honeymoon." He winked and they went their separate ways.

Helen wrote to Bud that night and told him all about Jack Kennedy. When Bud received her letter, he felt a huge, ugly amount of jealousy creep into his bones. He shook with emotion. It went to the core of his being and it verged on hatred. Bud ran to the gym and shot baskets full force for two hours. That only dissipated about half of his feelings. Then he pulled out his emergency stash of cookies and ate all of them until his jealousy was well buried.

Two weeks later it was Helen's last week at her job there. Helen had been the Homecoming Queen at Asgood College with no close contenders. She was a beautiful woman with her hair glowing like mahogany. Her narrow nose was the envy of any plastic surgeon because there was no way it could be replicated. Her blue eyes were bright as polished aquamarine with a warmth behind them that could melt marshmallows. Her figure was like an hourglass enhanced with breasts that begged not to be contained. This was 1947. It wasn't 1969 where one would have thought going without a bra was part of The Declaration of Independence.

So in the summer of 1947 Helen was like the night waiting for a firefly as she worked in a hotbed of testosterone at Wright Field. A flight was arriving and she was ready to greet it as it was her job. She had worked up some fresh questions for these military men that would make them smile at her and give her good quotes for the base newspaper. She slashed on her lipstick and started to hurry out of the door.

The door was blocked by the large Colonel Collins. She knew he wasn't making a move on her. She didn't know what he was doing.

"Sir, the plane is here..."

"I know that, darling. You don't have to greet this one."

Helen's reporter reflexes were flexing. What was so special about this one?

"I am supposed to be out there, sir."

"There's nothing out there. I don't see or hear anything out there." His voice was flat.

"I do."

"You wouldn't want to be escorted down to the infirmary, now would you? We may have to check out your hearing and eyesight."

"My hearing is fine. I just heard the plane shut down."

Helen realized there was a scoop here. It was not like her to disobey disguised orders. Something in her had to know. She did not like the Colonel's tone with her either.

Helen should have, but she didn't think it through as she took her spike heel and jammed it into the Colonel's knee. She slapped her pad of paper across his face and took off towards the plane. As soon as the Colonel recovered from her 4F place kick, he chased after her. It was too late. Helen had already seen it.

Helen raced over to the gurneys being lifted off the plane. Now she wished she had not defied the Colonel. These were not soldiers. They were not human. These beings were emitting a low pitched hum. Their heads were large and out of proportion to their bodies. Their skin texture looked like a rooster after its feathers were plucked.

The being's eyes were huge and in the shape of inverted tear drops. They literally flashed. Helen's eyes met one being's eyes and felt an elevator descending sensation in her midriff accompanied with some static electricity. She looked away. Were these beings the injured from nuclear bomb experiments? Hoping to make a connection she greeted them with, "Hello." There was no response from the beings.

"See. I told you that you wouldn't be able to get an interview." The Colonel and his anger were behind her. "You may be a civilian, but you can't assault an officer like they are the enemy."

Helen was mortified. She whimpered. "I'm sorry. If I had only known...Who are these...these..."

"This is classified information. You are not supposed to know this...or see these aliens..."

Helen's reporter mode jumped in again. "Aliens? Like from outer space?"

"Go back to the office, young lady. You may be the first civilian court martial that ends in death." The Colonel barked like a dog that had swallowed a rabbit.

Helen knew he meant it. She glanced one more time at the beings to take one last mental picture and scurried to the office. Helen was the most frightened she had ever been in her life and it wasn't coming from the beings. Where was her fear of the Colonel when she had needed it?

The Colonel was livid. His knee felt like it had been bashed in with a banjo. Why had he picked this day of all days to go without caffeine or nicotine?

None of these were good factors for Helen. She was sequestered in a room that took two locked doors to get to it.

The Colonel decided to consult with his superiors including Helen's reporting officer the Three Star General. They came up with a plan that they thought was humane yet would not compromise national security.

The next thing she knew Helen had a Coke® set in front of her. The Three Star General encouraged her to drink it and relax. The he left. He had not told her that the Coke® was laced with more than sugar. It was the same substance used to knock out the short term memories of the three suits.

Besides being smart Helen had good instincts. She knew the Coke® was not the innocent drink it should be. Helen took it and poured it on the brown carpet. She distributed it evenly in the four corners. Then her acting ability came into play. She feigned sleep. No one checked on her until the next morning. The Three Star came and roused her. Helen pretended like it was difficult to wake up.

Helen was asked what she had done the last twenty-four hours. She said her memory was fuzzy, but she thought she had a story to finish. After being asked a few more questions, it was determined that she could be given clearance.

The Colonel was informed that all was well. He was ready to forget all this grief and have a Coke® himself.

At the end of the summer Bud and Helen married. It was a simple and small wedding, but the ceremony was beautiful. They were married in the church which wasn't the custom in 1947. They honeymooned at Niagra Falls which was the custom in 1947. Not having much money they watched their funds carefully.

They had both graduated with honors from Asgood College. The Chancellor had taken notice of both Helen and Bud early on. He knew they were struggling financially. He was able to get Helen a job at a local radio station. Her Drama degree would be useful there.

Helen was thankful for the opportunity, but she dreamed of being a Hollywood actress. Bud did not know how deep this ambition was in her. She wanted to wait until her timing was right until she broached the subject with Bud. Being among palm trees was a different scenario than being among pastures.

The Chancellor had many contacts. He called Bud into his office. "Bud, you are the most natural born people person I have ever known. Everyone you meet likes you. It's a gift that shouldn't be wasted. Sales would be perfect for you. I know a fellow from a publishing company who is looking for a textbook salesman. Are you interested?"

"I'll have to talk it over with Helen."

Bud talked it over with Helen. Silently her dream was beginning to erode. Bud's enthusiasm for his employment possibility was obvious. Helen could take a back seat to his ambitions. Who knew where her radio job might lead?

Bud made it look easy to be hired by the book company. He studied the products diligently and read the Dale Carnegie book How to Win Friends and Influence People. He went out on the Ohio roads and called on elementary schools in his big territory. Principals were open to this young, persuasive salesman who was a natural. He made sale after sale which he credited to the product's excellence. There were nights that he had to stay over in motels due to the distances he traveled. He took to the work like a dog to a mailman.

Helen found how much she liked radio work. She was given her own talk show and became expert at creating sound effects to emphasize the points she was making. She didn't know it, but one of her best sound effects that listeners tuned in for was her wind chime laugh.

After three years of working Helen sublimated her drama dreams into motherhood. She was pregnant. Helen became a card carrying member of the Baby Boom. It was 1950. Helen and Bud's first child was a boy.

They named him Matt. He had black hair like his father and blue eyes like his mother. Matt was a good baby with good parents. They doted on him and began a photo album. They were a happy family. Bud was hoping for his son to be decent at playing basketball.

Two years later Matt had a baby sister. She was named Mollie. Mollie's eyes were blue too. She had a gurgling laugh which Bud wondered if it would turn into the sound of wind chimes. Mollie was a happy baby and her smile was a contagion.

During Helen's pregnancy with Mollie Helen thought a lot about the aliens she had seen. In fact, she obsessed about the incident. Later, she wondered if that had something to do with Mollie's obsession with flight. As an adult a psychiatrist told Mollie that she was "sensitized" to noticing airplanes.

Helen had never told anyone about what she had seen. She contemplated telling Bud, but was afraid that he might go around telling everyone. That would put their family in peril or put them in the position of being the town's laughing stock.

Mark was born two years after Mollie. He had his mother's mahogany hair and blue eyes. Mark was the most inquisitive of the three children and had to be watched so he would not pull on lamp cords or put shoes in his mouth. His smile could melt chocolate.

All three children had blue eyes like Helen. They did not have Bud's brown eyes.

As the expression goes, these three children "grew like weeds." Helen and Bud encouraged each of them to be their own person. As parents they were ahead of their time and stressed how it was a bad idea to drink, smoke, or use drugs. Most amazingly their children listened to them and honored their parents' wishes.

Each child was unique. Matt was a baseball fan. Later in life Mollie claimed that her brother was "a baseball fan until he went central air." Matt got Mollie interested in collecting baseball and football cards. Mollie was more interested in the bubble gum that came with them. They watched the Cleveland Indians on TV as well as Jimmy Brown bolt down the football field. Bud coached Matt's Little League team.

Mollie liked to ride her bicycle and pretend she was flying. She had a flair for the dramatic and performed magic tricks for the family. Matt claimed that he knew how she did her tricks. He was secretly frustrated at not knowing how they were done. Mollie was always feeling full of energy and that she was bursting with happiness. Her other hobby was collecting jokes. She dearly loved dogs.

Mark was the one taking things apart and putting them back together again. He had a natural gift for this. He was a sports fan as well. Whereas Mark had a flash temper, Mark was more laid back.

All three children had a tremendous sense of humor. They were skilled at making a pun and then building pun after pun on it. Their future spouses would helplessly witness this while rolling their eyes.

"This coffee has no grounds for being served."

"There you go spouting off again."

"I'm filtering what you are saying."

"Things are looking cup."

"Even though things are brewing."

"That might cause things to stir..."

Then the three siblings would erupt in laughter and groans.

Shortly after Mark was born, the family moved to Kent, Ohio so Bud would be more centrally located in his sales territory.

This was 1956 and Kent had not established its place in infamy yet. It was a town of family values, tree-lined streets, and rare black squirrels. People gathered on their front porches in the evening because television viewing was limited to only three channels.

When Mollie grew up, she was fond of saying that, "I had a good childhood and not a great adulthood."

In the winter Bud and Helen's children went sledding, ice skating, and had snowball fights. Bud fashioned a snowman in the shape of a teddy bear much to the delight of his kids.

In the summer there was swimming at a lake out in the country. There were trips to the library. The children spent a lot of time in the fresh air. At night fireflies were caught by Matt, Mollie, and Mark and put in Mason jars. They covered the jars with aluminum foil which they had punched holes in. In the morning they were released outside after the sleepover.

One night Helen heard screams from Mollie's bedroom. Bud and Helen rushed into her room and found escaped fireflies floating all over the room. Bud and Helen recaptured them. It didn't take much to convince Mollie to release them outdoors right away.

Soon after this Helen awoke screaming. She began having nightmares. They occurred every night. She went downstairs and warmed up milk. It didn't help. Helen went out on the front porch. The fireflies were tucked in for the night. She gazed up at the sky.

Bud came to check on her. "Sweetheart, what were you dreaming about?"

Helen swept back her hair. "I'm having nightmares about creatures from outer space."

Bud tried to reassure her. "That's about as possible as us landing on the moon." He laughed.

The wind chimes were silent.

CHAPTER 5

John Kendrick's academic record showed outstanding performance at The University of Chicago. He was not so fortunate at love. By 1959 he had been turned down for marriage three times. He decided he was asking the wrong women.

1959 became a luckier year for him, but in the areas of work and friendship. He was hired by the same publishing company that employed Bud Skilss. They met in the spring of 1959 at a state sales conference.

They hit it off immediately. Both men were gregarious and good at their jobs. Their sales territories were next to each other. Surprisingly their similarities ended there. John was a hard drinking, chain smoking agnostic who was a bachelor. Bud was a teetotaler, nonsmoker, churchgoing family man. However, their personalities meshed for reasons God would not explain.

At home Bud talked incessantly about John. Helen's curiosity grew the more she heard about him.

"Do you think that he is someone the children should be around?" asked Helen.

"He has good sense and a heart of gold. I think he will be good around our family."

"Let's invite him for dinner."

That was an invitation that would eventually change everything.

===

Mollie's third grade teacher brought a radio to class. Her students listened on May 5th, 1960 as Alan Shepard soared briefly into space and splashed down into Mollie's awed imagination. Mollie was aware of a dream forming to become the first female astronaut! Her first flight pattern that she mastered was John Glenn's as Mollie navigated her yo-yo around three full circles with a flawless landing (nothing broke in the house).

The Nixon-Kennedy election pounced onto the scene in 1960. As if her opinion counted, Mollie proudly sported a Nixon campaign button that Bud had given her.

She wore it to school. While waiting in the foyer with loads of other kids, Mollie began chanting, "Kennedy in the bathtub; Nixon pulled the plug; down went Kennedy; glug, glug, glug."

A bigger kid knocked her button off just as the bell rang and it ended up being trampled on the floor as a kind of metaphorical portent to 1974.

After school Mollie returned home to her house which was brown shingled like the chocolate morsels that Helen baked into her oatmeal cookies. She headed for the Humpty Dumpty cookie jar because she needed some comfort food.

Helen was busy in the kitchen. "Mollie, I don't want you to spoil your dinner. We are having company tonight and I'm fixing something special. We are going to have Chocolate Refrigerator Cake for dessert and I know you want to save room for that."

"Who is the company?" In Mollie's kid mind she thought company meant a business like a cereal company.

"He is a friend of your father's. They work together."

It sounded boring to Mollie. Maybe she could do some magic tricks for him.

A couple of hours later John arrived larger than life with Bud. The first thing that Mollie noticed about him was his smile and the yo-yos he had brought for her and her two brothers.

John was immediately comfortable with these three cute, well behaved kids. It seemed natural that they lapsed into calling him John for the rest of his life. He did not seem like a "Mister" to them.

During dinner John was warm, funny, and entertaining. The children silently enjoyed his company and the special dinner. They observed him closely and knew that they wanted him to come back. Their parents were happy around him too.

John became a frequent guest. The children were fascinated by his cigarettes. He taught Mark how to light a match. By holding a cigarette lit end up and poking the air up and down, John tutored them on how to make smoke rings. John brought toys for each child whenever he visited. Mollie especially liked the chocolate cigarettes he brought. Mark was disappointed that he could not put a match to them.

John taught the children how to do the new dance called "The Twist." He told them to pretend that they were extinguishing a cigarette on the ground by moving their one foot around. At the same time they were to pretend they had a towel behind them that they were pulling back and forth sideways.

His sense of play was only topped by his sense of humor. He read them a story from the newspaper. "A woman in Chicago had her beloved pet cocker spaniel die at Thanksgiving time. She called a pet cemetery that said they would bury it if she brought it there. She wrapped her dead dog in newspaper and went to the bus stop with her bundle. At the bus stop two guys accosted her. One guy said to the other, 'Let's go. I've got the turkey.' Off they ran with the woman's bundle."

Then John let loose with his loud laugh punctuated with a cigarette cough. He was happy around this family.

John built a cottage in Michigan soon after this. It wasn't any old cottage. It was high on a sand bluff overlooking Lake Michigan. It was secluded and special. He lived there with his mother in the summer and the fall.

The Skilss family was invited to visit. Everyone thought they had landed in heaven.

Inside the radio played its relaxed tunes from the forties. Helen stopped in her tracks as "In the Mood" was broadcast. The grownups played Scrabble® as the radio provided its background music. When Mollie became older, she took her place at that melodic Scrabble® table.

As far as Mollie was concerned, this place ranked above movies and ice cream. She was given all the Pepsi Cola® she could drink. She and her two brothers spent most of the day on the beach at the base of the bluff. They tossed a ball to each other and floated on inner tubes as a kind of remedial surfing. John would sometimes bring out his small sailboat and give the children a ride. At night everyone would flock around a beach campfire and revel in this choice nature spot. Then everyone went back up the steep bluff to John's cottage. He had already hauled down his flags: Old Glory and a bright flag lettered "Don't Tread On Me" which pictured a coiled up snake.

Mollie would make herself a totally limp heap on the wicker sofa where she would be on the verge of sleep as she half heard the grownups talking earnestly about politics and other important matters. Then she drifted off into another place.

As soon as the sun hit the horizon in the morning, Mollie and her brothers raced back to the beach to make sure it was still there in its full grandeur. The grownups didn't make it there until late afternoon when the grains of sand were no longer glowing embers. The children walked far down the beach to a four story tall sand dune. They scuffled up the back of it which was like climbing up the Sphinx. Then they charged down the front of it by skiing on the sand with their bare feet. It was always over too quickly. It didn't matter because this was a place where a person lost all consciousness of time. Everything flowed. Watches weren't needed. The children repeated their ski run.

The children would return and sit on John's screened porch. Mollie poured another Pepsi® down. She had not had half as many martinis that John had consumed that day. His olive count was high. Fittingly he had christened his sailboat "Bottoms Up."

John would let out a roaring, hacking laugh as he made a witty putdown of the Kennedys. Sometimes he would just say, "Oh, those Kennedys" and laugh.

John's mother would shuffle out to the porch to make sure everyone was being spoiled enough. Estrella had meringue white hair that matched her anklets. Her voice quavered which seemed to go along with her small steps.

However, when getting into the car with her, she made Mario Andretti look like he had training wheels. Mollie rode with her once and thought the car was inches away from flying.

Estrella's kitchen was her refuge and her strength. Estrella was the epitome of hospitality. Her meals were tasty and always topped off with freshly sliced peaches with brown sugar crowned with a plop of sour cream. It hit the spot after all of those sweet Pepsis.®

****

The guests were gone. John sat alone on his screened in porch. He could hear the waves rolling onto shore below him. He was wearing his Hawaiian print shirt and swim trunks. John was in a thinking mood. This morning he had already thought up a name for his special place: Sanwadoon. It was a combination of part of the words "sand," "water" and a variation of "dune." John went and poured himself a martini to celebrate his creativity.

As he drank it, his trusty German Sheperd was by his side. Isabella had been a stray on the beach and John had taken her in. He liked to brag, "Isabella is the only true Christian I know."

Something else was on John's mind today, but he didn't know what. He didn't believe in reincarnation, but he was having bits and pieces of what seemed like memories. These were very strong when he was out on the water with his sailboat. John mentioned it to his mother and Estrella said she had experienced the same thing when she took flying lessons years before this.

John sold books for a living, so he naturally believed a book might have the answers he was hunting. He went to a small bookstore in town. He combed through it. He considered books on reincarnation and then proceeded to the psychiatric manuals. John knew this sounded crazy. As he was in the psychology section, John found what might be helpful. It was a book on self-hypnosis. In John's mind that would be much more practical than finding out he was a trout in his past life.

Isabella met John at the door. Estrella had three of her friends over and they were playing a spirited game of mahjong. John went out to the porch and began studying his new book. What he didn't know was that it wasn't just a book. It was a can of worms.

The next night John decided to hypnotize himself. He closely followed the instructions in the book. First, he lit a candle and he stared into its flame. Then he began giving himself hypnotic suggestions. Soon he was in a trance.

John lost all awareness of time. He pulled out of the trance. There was a feeling of unreality. He had a large amount of recall, but it was shadowed by his disbelief. Lighting a cigarette he went into the kitchen and made a martini. This time he made it a double.

John discounted the experience. It was his imagination talking---not reality. Plastic surgery? Joseph Kennedy Jr.? He was a Republican for God's sake. John poured himself another drink. This marked the point where he began chain smoking and chain drinking.

John did consult a physician about whether he had plastic surgery on his nose. The physician thought it was odd that John would not know this. John came up with a clever and convincing story so the physician indulged him. It turned out that John had a nose job in the past, but it was to make his nose bigger.

This was a bizarre puzzle for John. He asked Estrella about his nose job and she did not have any recollection of any such thing. His own mother would certainly know that this was done.

John needed to talk to someone about this. A psychiatrist would only try to talk him out of it, diagnose him, prescribe medication, and present him with a hefty bill. Estrella had gone through a deep depression years prior and all it got her was being zapped with ECT. Since he had never been to church, he guessed a priest would sprinkle holy water on him. He smiled to himself as he came up with his last alternative: writing to Dear Abby. Of course he didn't do this, but decided to keep his secret to himself for now.

The Skilss family came to visit a month later. While the children played on the beach, Bud decided to read on the porch. He wasn't fond of sand and water. John and Helen went down to the beach and waded in the water lapping ashore. The two of them walked down the beach. Isabella romped beside them.

They talked about the children. John was genuinely interested in how they were doing. Then they talked about Estrella and whether her depression had subsided.

Their conversation came easily. They enjoyed each other's company. It was completely innocent. It was like a brother and sister relationship and little did they know that it was.

Helen self-disclosed first. "I have been having nightmares. They are terrifying and I am losing a lot of sleep."

John leaned over to pick up a shell. "Have you ever tried a martini before bed?"

"You know better than that. This is almost driving me to drink."

"I've been having trouble sleeping too," said John. "What are your nightmares about?"

"About creatures from space." Helen splashed a toe in the water. It felt warm.

"My insomnia has to do with a secret I have." John skipped a stone across the water and it made five leaps into the air. "I need to talk to someone about it."

"If you do, it won't be a secret anymore. It will be a burden shared by two people instead of one. I might start having more nightmares."

John kicked the sand. "Sharing a secret is the ultimate in trust. It is pure truth. I really would like you to know this about me. There's nothing you will have to do except listen. If you want to tell Bud someday, that is up to you. I wouldn't want to have anything come between you in your marriage like a secret."

Helen stopped walking and gazed far off into the distance where the water met the sky. "I'm already keeping something from Bud."

John knew better than to speak at that moment. He felt the water swirl around his ankles.

"It could be life or death if I told Bud my secret," said Helen. "He might not keep the confidence."

"It would be an honor for me to share my secret with you, Helen. You don't have to tell me yours."

They began walking again. Isabella had dug a hole in the sand while they had talked about divulging secrets. Dogs have a myriad of secrets. For starters, no one knows what they are thinking.

"It is a good thing to share a load," said Helen. "If you think it would be helpful to talk about it, then let me in on your secret."

They climbed the sloping sand dune and sat at the top like it would afford extra privacy. John lit a cigarette and even though he knew better, he offered one to Helen.

She declined. Helen could share in his secret, but not in his tobacco.

John started. "This is going to sound bizarre and I have no solid proof. For a long time I have felt a sense of unreality about myself.   There were feelings that I would call trace memories where things reminded me of feelings that might be left over from the past. This is going to sound crazy."

"If it sounds crazy, it doesn't mean it isn't true." Helen knew this personally.

That comment gave John the courage to continue. "I bought a book on hypnotism. It was fascinating. So I hypnotized myself."

"Did you act like a chicken?" The wind chimes sounded.

John did his hacking laugh. "It surprised me. It turns out I am Joe Kennedy Jr." Then John related how his appearance had been altered.

"Why?" wondered Helen.

"I know it doesn't make much sense."

"Are you going to try to find out more?"

"No. There must be a good reason. As you say, it could be a life or death situation for me and others if people knew this."

"Does this mean you will quit making fun of the Kennedys?"

"No, I'm a diehard Republican."

They sat in silence while John finished his cigarette. Helen's mind was churning. She respected John highly yet this latest tale bordered on fantasy. Helen stopped herself. After all, her experience with the space aliens that summer sounded farfetched too. The unknown could not always be explained.

John spoke again. "I like my life. Fame is not something I would thrive on. That's why I like Sanwadoon. It guards my privacy."

"I've always wanted to be hypnotized."

"Let me see your eyes," John said. He peered into her blue eyes. "You would be a good subject."

"You have to promise not to probe into my nightmares."

"Isn't that something that would help you?"

"I'm more interested in finding out if I'm someone else too."

"Do you want to do it now?"

Helen agreed. She covered her toes with sand. John easily put her in a trance.

Secrets and hypnosis are both the ultimate in trust and responsibility. They are paths to the unexpected.

John was not prepared for what Helen revealed. He brought her out of the trance. He chain smoked three cigarettes in a row before he could tell Helen what he had found out. No wonder they clicked. They were blood relatives. This was incredible.

"I feel well rested," said Helen. "What happened?" She felt that waiting through three cigarettes was long enough.

"This is going to sound like a theme song," said John. He looked at her eyes that he never realized how much they looked like his until now. "You are Kathleen Kennedy, my sister."

Suddenly Helen thought a martini might be a good idea---with three olives.

CHAPTER 6

Bud thrived as a book salesman. He stopped at schools during the day and spent his time there charming the principals. The principals liked him and they bought his books.

Because schools were not in session during the summer, Bud didn't work during the summer. This became family time. One summer the family traveled to Washington, D.C. Another time they drove to Florida in their oil burning Nash Rambler. Bud poured oil into the car for the entire trip because they were determined not to have their trip spoiled. The cars following them might have had their trips spoiled from the Rambler's fumes. In Florida they swam in the ocean, went to Marineland, and went to an alligator park. Mollie thought this was the best place she had ever been and wondered why they weren't living here.

Bud's success did not escape notice from the corporate offices outside Chicago. He was offered a promotion.

This was a major decision. The family was well established with friends and their church in the community. They were comfortable.

Bud was ambitious. Helen could not make up her mind. She wanted to support her husband in this opportunity, but thought their family would be better off staying in Kent. It was also a matter of the familiar versus the unfamiliar.

Bud's skills as a salesman came into play. He was able to sway Helen, but her doubts remained with her. She didn't talk about them.

In August, 1962 the Skilss family packed up and set off for Chicago with the moving van trailing behind them. Their station wagon was stashed with suitcases. Mark's turtle bowl with its turtle suspended in the water was perched precariously on top of the suitcases. Like Helen, the turtle wasn't sure about this moving stuff either.

Helen clung to her ambivalence. The lump in her throat would dissolve into tears later that night when she was not around the children.

The Skilss family moved to the North Shore of Chicago. Like it sounds, it is north of the city of Chicago and borders Lake Michigan. They were settling into one of the exclusive villages.

This village was an enclave for the wealthy. Ethel Kennedy was originally from there. The Wrigleys lived here. In later years Phil Donahue and Marlo Thomas would live here. Millionaires proliferated like mosquitoes.

A lot of mansions covered the town. Many were near the Lake. The Northwestern commuter train sliced through the village so there was "a right side to to the tracks," but there were "right areas" among the "wrong side of the tracks."

The Skilss found a small rental house. It was too pricey here for them to buy. They had not sold their Kent house yet. Bud's salary would barely cover their expenses. It was going to be a major adjustment. Helen felt sick to her stomach. The stress of making ends meet daunted her.

There were tradeoffs. The village had canopies over the streets provided by the old elms. Most of the streets were named after trees. Lake Michigan was beautiful. Uptown had quaint little stores including Charlie's which was a variety store with everything from wax lips to goldfish bowls. Trees dotted the streets in the uptown area too. The Sweet Shop where ice cream was dipped out like love was also uptown. Fred's Bicycle Shop, The Toy Shop, and Betty's of Winnetka lined the streets. The Village Green was not too far away where Congressman Donald Rumsfeld would read the Declaration of Independence on the Fourth of July.

On the other side of town was the Nielsen Tennis Center that the Nielsen family of TV ratings had donated to the village. The sledding hill was a testament to snow and a lawsuit waiting to happen. Children eyed it like a mountain. Close by were an eighteen hole and par three golf courses.

The schools were considered to be the best in the nation. The place looked flawless. All this was there for its population of 13,500.

It might have been picture perfect, but its beauty was only surface deep. Per capita per square mile this village had the highest suicide rate in the country at the time. Inwardly its residents could not keep up its appearance.

Helen was not ambivalent about living here. She detested it. Missing the homeyness of Kent was part of it. The other part had to do with feeling she did not fit in. These people were wealthy and she did not come close to that.

The house bothered Helen too. It was cramped and their furniture was jammed into all the rooms. It felt like a trap to Helen. She and the furniture were caged animals.

Helen was grieving. During the day waves of crying bouts washed over her. In the evening she tried to be strong for Bud and the kids.

There is no timetable for grieving. Helen's grief lasted for the next two or three years. What didn't help was that there was talk that Bud might be transferred to Dallas. Helen didn't want to get too settled in this new place because the family might be uprooted again. She felt up in the air without a balloon.

Her days were miserable. The children would often see her staring out of the kitchen window. Helen's days held little joy. She cleaned the house, did the grocery shopping, cooked, reviewed their abysmal finances, and wished she were back in Kent.

Two or three times a year the family returned to Ohio. The family was happiest on these trips. In the car they sang songs and rounds like "Little Tommy Tinker" and "I Love the Mountains." These pilgrimages were always too short. Helen tried to hide her inner moroseness when they left.

The family sing-a-longs around the piano ceased. Helen did not play for the joy of it anymore. She gave up gardening which she had done in Kent to keep a colorful flower bed in blossom all spring and summer. The North Shore was not home to her.

Bud was enthusiastic about his work. He found every day to be stimulating. He was at the main office and there were many other employees around. Bud was good at getting to know others without talking about himself. This curiosity about others had made him a good salesman and now it was paying off for him politically. He got along well with others and this was noted by his superiors. Bud was regarded as a potential leader.

After work Bud would go home and tell Helen all about his day as she fixed dinner. He asked her advice about different work matters and Helen volunteered her opinion. She did enjoy this part of the day, but it didn't last long enough. Bud would change out of his suit and tie so that he could sit down and read the paper.

Bud was aware how miserable Helen was feeling. It dampened his high spirits about his job.

Helen brought it up on one low day. "Bud, I'm happy for you, but I don't know how long I can stand it here."

Bud tried to reason with Helen, but this was an emotional issue and not something to think through. "What is not to like here?"

"The house for starters. We don't have a church. Everything is temporary. We might have to leave here and go to Dallas! I don't have friends. My life isn't interesting. You escape by going to work. You fit in at work. I don't fit in here."

Bud knew it was the wrong thing to say as soon as it left his mouth. "Should we get a dog?"

Helen sobbed. Bud realized that he couldn't recall the last time he heard the wind chimes. He thought he might have heard them in response to his dog joke.

"Let me take you out Saturday night. We will go into Chicago."

Helen whimpered. "We can't afford that."

Bud wrapped his arms around her waist. "Yes, we can. I've been saving up the allowance you've been giving me."

Helen smiled weakly. "You don't want to put it towards a poodle?"

Matt was taking to the new community like a squirrel to an acorn. He was a new seventh grader in his middle school. The other students had a welcoming curiosity towards him. He captured their acceptance.

Sometimes popularity status is conferred on the new kid in school.

Besides being new at school Matt had the charisma of his father. Matt was elected to be a Student Council member. His grades were outstanding and being a model student earned him points with his teachers. By throwing himself into his homework he was able to make a good adjustment all around.

It helped that he had a trio of friends to spend time. Jake was a cute, blonde haired kid who was smart and personable like Matt. His father was a physician, but Jake had already decided that was too much to live up to in his goals. Jake always had a smile on his face like he was laughing at his own private joke. Jake was the one of the four of them who had great ideas for things to do. One of his best ideas was to take his family's sailboat out on Lake Michigan. They ended up in the water and ended up having a great time.

Sam was another one of the trio of friends. He was Jewish which the friends couldn't have cared less about than if he had been a goat that blew up balloons. Sam had a tremendous sense of humor and could make them all laugh. He was also the best trumpet player in the school. Matt and Sam were the most outgoing of the four.

Andy was Jewish too. He was the studious one with glasses and a serious look. Andy was more on the shy side than the others. He was flattered to be included in this small group of friends. What he saw as his role was to recognize the good in each friend and point this quality out to each boy just enough to remind them not only of their good, but his good too.

Matt had the support system that his mother did not have. If Helen had such friends, she might have coped better.

Mark did not have the luxury of a friend either. He had a megaphone mouth that loudly spouted off to the other kids at school. Mark was obnoxious and kids began to pick on him. These verbal assaults deteriorated into physical assaults. Mark was not a skilled fighter since his only weapon his mouth was insufficient. The Jewish boys knocked him down, sat on him, and demanded, "Christian or Jew?" before they freed him.

Mark drowned his sorrow in food. Cheese curls became his best buddy as he laid on the couch in the summer and watched The Chicago Cubs. There were some neighbor kids with whom he got along and with whom he played. Bud hung a tire swing on the elm tree at the side of the house which acted like a magnet for other children who might be around. Mark and Mollie depended on each other to play games together since Matt had his own circle of friends.

Mark, Mollie, and Helen were the ones fighting off loneliness and withdrawal pangs from Kent. They didn't talk about it; they hurt in silence.

Before moving to the North Shore Mollie was a superior reader. After the move she began to read very slowly and had to reread sentences over and over. She wasn't comprehending anymore. School was a struggle. She had gone from having many friends in Kent to having none on the North Shore. Mollie became very quiet. At night she wept.

She developed insomnia. The insomnia was caused by her ant farm. The ant farm was a Christmas gift. She sent her certificate in for her ants after Christmas. In the dead of winter the ants arrived dead in a plastic tube. Finally the company sent her live ants. She dumped them into her plastic ant farm and watched them tunnel. She began having trouble sleeping because she was afraid the ants would escape.

As Mollie lay awake at night, she also thought about having friends. She wanted to be popular. It was so out of reach for her. Matt was popular. Why couldn't she? Mollie was in the dark as she lay in the dark. She did not like to be left out. She was a decent, nice person who could be a good friend. Mollie craved popularity which ultimately led to her undoing.

She decided she needed a way to gain acceptance and what better way to do this than to tell a joke. One day at recess she was surrounded by five other girls. She launched into a story she had tediously read in a folklore book.

"There was this guy who worked on a ship. The captain told him to do some work. Instead, the guy said he was working on a Kluuug machine. The next day the captain told him to swab the deck. The guy said he couldn't because he was working on his Kluuug machine. The day after that the captain asked him to fix breakfast for the crew. The guy said he was still working on the Kluuug machine. The captain said he wanted to see the Kluuug machine the next day and it must work."

Mollie looked around at the five girls. She had their attention. They were hanging onto her every word. It felt good not to be ignored.

"The next day the guy brought the Kluuug machine on deck. The machine had dials, cords, switches, and gauges all over it. The captain asked to see how it worked."

"The guy leaned over the side of the ship and dropped the machine." Mollie raised her voice for the punchline.

"When it hit the water, it went **KLUUUG!**"

Mollie had never seen five girls run away like that. They could not get out of her presence fast enough.

Mollie did not put that one into her joke file. She should have stuck with a shorter joke she liked which was, "How do you top a tar?"

The punchline? "You tep on the brake, tupid."

Besides jokes, Mollie's other passion was dogs. Unlike her parents she wanted a dog quite badly. It would have helped her loneliness. In the meantime, she began a short lived dog walking business. The neighbors had two Bassett Hounds that she walked for a quarter.

It was the spring of 1963. Helen had not warmed up to the locale at all. Mollie was in the sixth grade and she and Mark were still not fitting in with their peers.

Bud was working diligently. He had already been promoted. He loved his work. One fateful day he received a phone call. Bud did not recognize the voice on the other end. The voice had a Texas drawl.

"This is the cowboy," the voice said.

"Who?"

"LBJ," said the voice.

Bud knew it was a joke. The Vice-President of The United States didn't know there was a Bud Skilss. Bud decided to joke back. "LBJ: Like Beautiful Jelly."

"I'm serious, Bud. This is the Vice President of the United States. I want to meet with you. I will send a limo for you tomorrow at work which will take you to O'Hare. Then you will fly to Texas to my ranch where we will meet.

I've arranged for you to take off work. You are not to tell anybody about whom you are going to see."

"What about my wife?"

"When you get back. There will be parameters."

Bud was in shocked silence.

"From now on I will only identify myself on the phone to you as 'the cowboy.' Adios."

The receiver went dead and Bud's imagination came alive. Maybe someone he knew recommended him for some government post because of his hard work and ability with people. Maybe LBJ just wanted to pick his brain. Maybe this had something to do with the possibility that had been talked about regarding a transfer to Dallas.

Bud did not get much work done for the rest of the day. He went home and told Helen that he was leaving for Texas the next day. She automatically assumed that the trip had something to do with Bud's possible transfer to Dallas.

"Bud, I don't know if I can get used to another place."

"You're not used to this place. Maybe Dallas will be more to your liking. You have to realize we will never move back to Kent. You look back so much that you are a pillar of salt."

Helen began weeping. "I wish I could be a pillar of strength. I miss my friends. I miss our old life. You have your work and your friends at work."

Bud hugged her. "I'm sorry," said Helen. "You just caught me at a weak moment."

"Honey, maybe things will change for the better soon. We'll talk more after I get back from Texas."

A limo picked up Bud and he was at O'Hare in twenty minutes. O'Hare was a crush of people and Bud had to pick up his pace to keep up with the flow of people.

A voice was paging passengers. Its amplification carried over all of the other airport sounds.

Bud checked in his one piece of luggage and wandered the corridors of this palatial airport. He spied a bank of telephones. Bud went over, put a dime in the phone, and dialed a number.

Helen answered. "Hello."

"I wanted to make sure you are o.k. Is there anything you want me to bring you back from Texas?"

"Anything but a transfer."

Bud knew she was serious. He decided to keep it light. "An armadillo it is. Love you."

"Love you too. Have a safe trip."

Bud chewed some gum. He needed to spare his ears on takeoff and landing.

He could only kill so much time. He was looking forward to this trip and meeting the Vice-President of the United States. What an honor.

Bud felt he was one lucky buckaroo. He leaned back in his seat on takeoff and daydreamed. He smiled to himself. If only he had a Stetson, he could tip his cowboy hat on meeting LBJ. Little did he know that he would not have this desire again.

CHAPTER 7

The plane touched down in Texas, but Bud's spirits were higher than the sky. Here he was deep in the heart of Texas. Helen would be so proud of him. Bud quickly picked up his luggage and a limo driver picked him up.

Bud was driven to Johnson City and then to the road leading to LBJ's ranch. The car turned into a road that was lined with trees. On the left side of the road ran the Pedernales River. The limo got to a point in the road where they were parallel to a dam in the river. The limo swerved and drove through the river on top of the dam.

"Whoa," said Bud not realizing the irony of his cowboy vernacular.

The road met them on the other side. The limo driver laughed. "Word has it that LBJ loves to scare folks by doing that."

Soon the limo pulled up to LBJ's white house with black shutters. It was shaded by trees. The main part of the house had a bay window protruding from the front. Columns supported a second floor balcony to the left of this.

Bud was mildly surprised. The houses on the North Shore (except for his) were much bigger and impressive than this one.

The limo zoomed off and the front door of the house opened. There was LBJ in a cowboy hat striding towards Bud.

"Howdy," said LBJ.

The men shook hands with equally firm grasps.

"Let me show you around," said LBJ.

The two of them walked over to an open overhang where there was a bunch of cars. LBJ motioned to Bud to climb into a white Lincoln convertible. A beagle wandered over.

"Do you mind if Little Beagle Johnson goes along with us?"

"As long as he doesn't drive."

LBJ lifted the other LBJ into the back seat and off they zipped. Bud wished the dog were driving. LBJ was flooring the car without letting up. He let out a whoop. "Yahoo!"

Their first stop was at a field full of Herefords. They were enclosed by a split rail fence. "Someday I'm going to have 400 head of these cattle. I'm well on my way."

LBJ also took Bud around to the family cemetery on the grounds and to the Show Barn.

"When I inherited this ranch, it was a dilapidated 250 acres. I will probably increase its acreage to 2700 acres by the time I die. You know all about dilapidated, don't you?"

Bud knew he was talking about his parent's farm. This guy had done his homework.

On the way back to the house Bud leaned over and pocketed a black walnut from the ground. LBJ had his back turned and did not see the souvenir being taken.

LBJ did not give Bud a tour of the house. Instead, they went into his study. The desk had a Remington statue on it. Bud went to sit down.

LBJ's tone of voice turned sharp. "Don't make yourself comfortable."

Both men were standing. LBJ went over and positioned himself two inches from Bud's face. Bud had never heard of "The Treatment" that LBJ was famous for doling out, but Bud was being the recipient of it.

Bud thought this was all odd. He hadn't even been offered any iced tea.

LBJ lowered his voice. It was soft. "You are going to do as I say."

Bud knew better than to respond, but what he wanted to say was that he gave up playing "Simon Says" a long time ago.

LBJ continued. "You are going to assassinate John F. Kennedy. There will be no money for you. Instead, there will be consequences if you don't do it."

Now LBJ had leaned in to be one inch from Bud's face. "If you don't kill him, we will take away your daughter. Mollie is her name, right?"

Bud grew cold. It felt like he was encased in an ice cube.

"Why me? We've never met."

"Son, that may be so, but I know you better than you know yourself."

It took everything for Bud not to try and bite this jerk's nose.

LBJ went on. "I don't care how you do it; just do it. Never mention that we have ever met. Make sure it's done by the end of the year. Now skedaddle. A car is waiting for you out front."

LBJ backed up after he purposely exhaled a big breath of fetid breath into Bud's face. LBJ opened up the study door. "Men."

Two gigantic men suddenly appeared and pushed Bud out the front door. Bud stood there as the chauffeur opened the car door. Bud swallowed hard. This had to be worse than any of Helen's nightmares.

After Bud was dropped off at the airport, he rented a car. He drove nonstop to Dallas. He stopped in at his company's regional headquarters. His colleagues showed him around town and went by The Texas School Book Depository where their company's books were stored. Bud tried to take everything in, but he was distracted.

At home Helen was brooding. She knew she shouldn't be keeping her secrets from Bud. Her marriage would be strengthened if she told Bud the truth. He would honor her privacy.

Helen could not get over the fact that she was The President of The United State's sister. This was bizarre. JFK certainly did not know this when they met twenty-six years earlier. Did he know now? What had happened that she and John Kendricks were hidden away like they had been? It was a kooky claim to make so it would have to be up to JFK to contact and acknowledge her. Helen was ready to unburden herself. She was looking forward to Bud's return.

Helen had an insight. Maybe her poor adjustment to the Chicago area had more to do with her suppression of secrets. It took a great deal of energy to stifle major issues. Helen was already feeling her load lighten. She decided to make Bud's favorite dinner. Helen began at once to make city chicken.

When Bud returned home, Helen thought he looked worn. She became more concerned when he picked at his city chicken and declined dessert.

Bud was wrestling with his own secret. He could not pin down what he should do.

"Honey, I'm going to take a long bath. Where do the kids keep their bubble bath?"

Helen thought how unlike this was for Bud. She decided not to push the issue. Helen also decided to keep her secrets for a while longer.

"I'll get it for you. Bubble baths are great for stress."

Bud was in the bubble bath for two hours. He kept refreshing the cooled down water with fresh hot water. He did some productive thinking. Tomorrow he would start putting his plan into action.

The next morning Helen noticed that Bud was more of himself yet she detected preoccupation in his eyes. Bud hugged her. "That urban chicken was delicious," he said.

"Because you didn't eat much of yours last night, we're having it again tonight," said Helen.

"Does that make it suburban chicken?" asked Bud.

"You can't take the city out of city chicken," said Helen. Helen was warming up like leftovers.

Bud left for work. At lunchtime he asked his colleagues about authentic Italian restaurants located in Chicago. Brett told him what he wanted to hear.

"This place is so genuine that the mob eats there and they probably own it. I wouldn't be surprised if they launder their money in a washing machine in the back."

Bud wanted to find a hit man. He figured that the mafia would be a good place to find one.

The following Saturday Bud took the el downtown. Then he got into a taxi and went to the recommended restaurant.

The restaurant was dark inside. It was lit like they were hiding something. The walls were flocked with red and black. White tablecloths covered the tables. Thick carpeting was on the floor.

Bud decided he should eat something. Someone had once told him that the best dish to always order in an Italian restaurant was the lasagna. Bud suddenly recalled one of his favorite jokes:

A really dumb guy wants to go to Italy. To prepare for this he learns Italian. One day he finally gets to Italy. He walks into a place and starts saying, "Spaghetti...Ravioli...Lasagna."

The Italian owner responds. "That's fine, but this is a hardware store."

Bud knew he was taking a terrible risk with this whole situation. The tough looking waiter came over and took Bud's order for lasagna. The waiter was aghast that Bud did not want any wine. Bud decided to acquiesce and ordered red wine even though he was a teetotaler. The restaurant was empty so Bud knew he could get away with his plan. He only got the wine to win over the waiter. He was going to need his help.

Even though the lasagna was the best that he had ever had, Bud found himself forcing it down. When the waiter was in the kitchen, Bud leaned over and poured his red wine into the red carpet underneath the table.

The waiter presented the bill. Bud made his move. "I need to see the Boss...and I don't mean your boss of this restaurant."

The guy played the dumb waiter role. "I don't know what you mean."

"You know, the top guy. The big Boss." Bud flourished a fifty dollar bill.

The waiter faltered. "Who are you?" The waiter knew Bud was not a Fed by the way he was dressed.

"My name is Bud and I have some business that only the Boss can help me do."

"Stay here. This may take some time. I'll send some cannoli out for you while you wait." He plucked the fifty from Bud's fingers before he could say, "Holy cannoli."

An hour and a half later the waiter revisited Bud. "Come with me." He took Bud into a back room which was dark.

Bud was grabbed under both arms which were pinned behind him. His wallet was jerked out of his pocket. There were at least three thugs in the room with him. One of them frisked Bud. Of course he had no weapons unless you counted passing excess gas. One of the thugs spoke.

"You tell anyone bout dis place and youse will be the special of the day. Capische?"

"It's my advantage not to," said Bud. That ice cube of fear was gripping him again.

The thugs propelled Bud towards another room. Bud could smell cigar smoke. The door was opened and a haze of smoke greeted him.

The thugs left and the door shut. Bud did not know the man in the room behind the desk, but later found out it was Sam Giacana, a Chicago mob boss.

"Would you like a cigar?"

Bud declined. He would not be able to hide it in the carpeting.

"What can I do for you?"

Bud stopped himself for a moment. This was really happening. It was distasteful. It was wrong. It was something where he had no other choice.

"I have to kill The President."

"The President of what?"

"JFK."

Sam was quiet. He knew how to use dramatic pauses effectively.

Bud continued. "Someone is blackmailing me. If I don't kill JFK, my daughter will be taken away from me. I was thinking you might have a hit man that I could contact. I don't have any money. Maybe something could be worked out. I'm desperate."

Sam coughed due to either the cigar or Bud's request. "We might be able to help you. Your timing is good. Did you know my daughter is involved with JFK? He's two timing her."

This was all news to Bud.

"You can help us with some of the logistics. As for money payoff, twenty percent of your salary goes to me for the next three years. You don't pay it; you don't live. Do we have a deal?"

Bud knew he had sold his soul to the devil at a discount rate.

November 22, 1963 dawned like any other and descended like no other. John F. Kennedy was assassinated in the early afternoon. Bud was not surprised when he heard the news in Illinois. He felt guilty and ashamed when the shooting was linked to The Texas School Book Depository.

Most everyone else in the world was surprised. Mollie's sixth grade teacher laid her head on her desk and cried. She moaned, "Why did it have to be Dallas?" The teacher was originally from Dallas.

The Skilss went to church that Sunday. On the drive home they learned that Oswald, the alleged assassin, was shot dead by a Texan named Jack Ruby. It was later established that Ruby had mob ties. Also, later in Mollie's life she realized that their family rarely listened to the radio to and from church.

Bud became a rising, shining star at work. Bud didn't think his promotions had anything to do with the assassination, but he wasn't sure. He did not understand how LBJ had heard of him in the first place. Meanwhile, the talk of him being transferred to Dallas had ceased.

Time passed quickly. Mollie was now in the eighth grade and her reading skills had returned. She had a couple of friends which overjoyed her.

Helen was happier too. She found a four bedroom center hall colonial house that she and Bud bought. Ironically it was white with black shutters like LBJ's house.

The Skilss family began to eat out occasionally. Sometimes on Sundays they dined at a local restaurant called The Indian Trail. Little did they know that one of its dishwashers would be infamous one day. The exception was that Bud would know.

CHAPTER 8

Mollie's quest for popularity did not quell when she entered high school. Her popularity had peaked earlier in the sixth grade when she rigged her classroom election to become President. Mollie selected four girls to be the classroom officers including herself as President. During Shop class she approached every girl in the classroom and had them promise to vote for her candidates. Since the boys were all in Home Economics at the time, they didn't know what was going on.

The election was a success. Mollie was now President, but she knew she really wasn't popular. She was just a good organizer.

In high school Mollie had her pattern of having a couple of friends. In Mollie's mind she pictured droves of friends. She was on the shy side so that was more unrealistic than she imagined.

Sophomore year reared its ugly head. Mollie figured that the surest and quickest way to become popular was to become a cheerleader. There were some drawbacks to this plan.

Mollie's voice did not project well. It might have been due to her small mouth. As an adult her dentist told her, "Remind me before you leave to give you exercises to make your mouth bigger."

Mollie had incredulously reacted. "You've got to be kidding!"

The dentist admitted he was, but never broke a smile.

The other drawback was that Mollie could not do a cartwheel. Her cartwheel looked more like a hunkered down spider. Mollie was hardly graceful or supple. She was meant more for field hockey. The Friday night before this Mollie was invited to a classmate's birthday party. Mollie had a good time, but years later she had a vague recollection that someone had said something evil about her father. As much as she tried to remember, it was as elusive as her popularity.

Mollie went home and was wound up more than if she had drunk a gallon of coffee. She went to bed and stared at where the ceiling should be in the dark. Mollie thought of the cheerleader tryouts and the instant popularity she would gain as a cheerleader. Then Mollie imagined what it would be like being popular short of signing autographs. Mollie felt currents of energy coursing through her body.

Anxiety took over from there. Mollie began to wonder if her cartwheel were passable. She had some insight that her cartwheel looked like a flat tire. Knowing what was at stake Mollie knew she had to go ahead. She did not sleep that night. She had not slept the previous two nights either.

Mollie got up early on Saturday. She silently ate breakfast with her family. The Skilss family ate every meal together.

The energy bursting within Mollie had not subsided. She wandered into the living room. A ghostly image materialized. Mollie felt like she was losing it and she was.

Helen came into the living room. Mollie looked at her and said, "I need help." What happened from there was a lost recollection for Mollie. What she did know later was that she did not have to perform her lopsided cartwheel and that she was doomed to be unpopular.

Mollie was hospitalized psychiatrically at the local asylum. The building had Alfred Hitchcock written all over it. It was made out of ancient bricks and was perched on the shore of Lake Michigan.

There was only one other teenager there. Darren was the same age as Mollie's older brother. Matt wasted no time in telling his parents that Darren used drugs.

This did not help Mollie's cause. Mollie's psychiatrist speculated to her parents that she had used drugs and that was what led to her hospitalization. This was 1968 and there were no urine tests to detect street drugs. At least this hospital didn't use them.

Helen and Bud felt sick. Like Mollie's cartwheel the family was turned upside down.

Helen felt like a failure as a parent. She went to her family doctor who prescribed Librium for her.

Mark felt bad too. He approached Helen and asked, "Why doesn't Mollie love me anymore?"

Sleep deprivation studies in the future determined that anyone will become psychotic after going seventy-two to one hundred straight hours without sleep. Mollie had gone at least seventy-two hours without any shut eye. A psychiatrist whom Mollie saw in adulthood told her that the first psychotic episode a person has can be quite severe and fragmented so as to look drug induced.

This was the first time Mollie had ever been away from home. She had always refused to go away to camp because she had heard stories about skinny dipping there and did not want to be a part of that.

Mollie's memories of this hospitalization were sparse. She was told that she had insulin shock therapy as well as electric shock treatment.

What Mollie remembered was more sensory. Her parents often came to the hospital in the evening and brought her homemade popcorn. Her dad made the best popcorn. It rivaled any movie popcorn.

When Mollie ate with the older women patients, they gave her their desserts. This meant Mollie had four desserts every night. She went home ten pounds heavier.

The sound of the ward door slamming shut was another of Mollie's memories. The door was made out of solid, thick steel. When it shut, its reverberation shook Mollie's insides like cascading nails.

Matt visited Mollie. They played Ping- Pong.™ Matt won of course. He was playing someone who couldn't do a cartwheel.

Darren and Mollie spent endless time playing a popular game in 1968 called Mille Bornes.™ Darren knew how to draw out Mollie and they became like brother and sister.

The insulin shock treatment seemed to be part of what worked. It consisted of giving Mollie injections of insulin in increasing doses to induce a coma. Then a seizure would ensue.

Mollie's day also consisted of sitting stunned in the semi-light dayroom. She kept quiet as if she were keeping a vigil for herself. In the evenings she perked up and towards the end of her stay she played Kings in the Corner with the other patients.

A month before Mollie was hospitalized Bud was concentrating hard at work. His phone rang.

"Hello."

"Is this Bud Skilss?"

"Yes."

"We want you to kill Martin Luther King Jr. If you don't, we will take away Mollie and Mark." The line went dead. Bud went dead inside.

Bud did not know who this was. He reasoned it could not be LBJ for two reasons. One reason was that he had not identified himself as "the cowboy." The second reason was that LBJ was a proponent for Civil Rights.

Being fed up with this and loaded with guilt Bud knew he needed help before he had a permanent part-time job arranging assassinations. He decided to contact the smartest person he knew. Bud grabbed the phone like it was a life preserver.

He dialed the phone and it rang until Bud almost gave up.

"Hello."

"Hi, John."

"Bud, good to hear from you. Did you get promoted again?"

"John, I need your help. I'm in a lot of trouble."

"Oh, did Helen tell you her secrets?"

"What are you talking about?" Bud was more aggravated than ever. It was beyond the aggravation he usually felt when doing crossword puzzles. Helen was keeping something from him. He was keeping something from her. What kind of marriage was this where his best friend was closer to Helen than he was?

"Where and when can we meet?" Bud forged on.

"This doesn't sound like it can wait. Come over to my apartment in Chicago tonight." The desperation in Bud's voice was a foreign sound to John.

As soon as work was over, Bud broke every speed limit and cut off a record number of drivers to get to John's place. John greeted him heartily. He asked about Helen and the kids. He poured a soda pop for Bud and sat down with his trademark martini. "Do you want an olive for your pop?" John asked.

Normally Bud would have laughed. The tension inside him was tauter than a tight wire.

Bud took a gulp of his soda. The fizz went up his nose. He had to pause which gave John an opening.

"I may not be the one to tell you Helen's secrets. I know one of them, but she did not divulge the other one. I'm sorry I said something."

"That's all right," said Bud. "We will clear the air when I get home. I haven't been one hundred per cent honest with her either. That isn't why I'm here."

"Oh?" John swished the olive around in his martini glass.

"I'm between the devil and the dark, blue sea."

"And you can't even swim." John was uncomfortable. He was making weak jokes.

"If you don't want to be burdened with a terrible secret, tell me now."

John knew he could keep a terrible secret. He was keeping his own. "That's o.k., Bud."

Bud stood up and paced over to the bar area. He poured himself another soda. "I got a disturbing phone call today."

John was thinking of more poor jokes, but had the good sense to keep quiet.

"I was told that if I didn't assassinate Martin Luther King Jr. that Mollie and Mark would be taken away from me."

John let this sink in like the alcohol he had imbibed. He needed more information. "What are you going to do?"

"Do I have a choice?"

"If you kill Dr. King, Mollie and Mark will be taken away from you anyway. More accurately you will be taken away from them. Dr. King will be lost too. Is that what you want?"

"What are my other choices?"

"You could go to the authorities."

"That may sound practical, but it's impractical."

"Why?"

"I don't know who is behind the threat." Bud crunched on an ice cube.

"Don't act out of fear. That's what they want. They are counting on you to be irrational." John skewered his olive and ate it in one bite.

"So what are you saying?"

"Don't do anything."

"That would put Mollie and Mark at risk!"

"You are taking a bigger risk if you kill Dr. King. You don't want to murder him." John thought better than to fix another martini at the moment.

John continued. "If you don't try to kill him, someone else will probably be set up to do it. If you get another call, just say it has been arranged. Don't offer any details. That way you will be given credit for it and your kids will be safe."

Bud slumped back in his chair. "I am so grateful for you."

"Next time I see you, bring me a jar of olives as a token of your gratitude."

They toasted their empty glasses.

On April 3, 1968 Mollie was discharged from the psychiatric hospital. She was heavier and rolled out of the asylum. She felt like the oversized stuffed animal that her homeroom had sent her.

School was going to be over for the summer in two months. Mollie had already missed a month and a half of her classes along with the cheerleading tryouts. Helen arranged for Mollie's teachers to come to the house to tutor Mollie.

Mollie's geometry teacher was the first tutor. As he babbled on about various theorems, Mollie realized her head was devoid of any memory of geometry. It was an emptiness like a hole in her head. Mollie could not fake past her ignorance and knew the teacher realized what she did not admit. He mercifully never returned and passed her for the course.

The English teacher was next. He was a Shakespeare nut. Mollie wasn't. She did not understand why he wrote so that no one (or at least Mollie) could understand what he was getting at. She read Macbeth under his tutelage and found it wasn't too bad.

Then her favorite teacher came to the house. She was Mollie's French teacher. Mrs. Saint was tough, but knew how to teach effectively. Mollie had almost grown a beret in her class. In the fall Mollie had gone to her and cried as she lamented her loneliness. Probably Mrs. Saint looked uncomfortable at the time because she was out of her element when it didn't involve the Eiffel Tower. Mollie couldn't recall Mrs. Saint's advice to her, but it was helpful to open up to someone.

Mrs. Saint was glad to see Mollie even though there was more to see of her. The two of them sat down at the family room table and Mrs. Saint started in on the lesson.

Mollie could not hide it. Her French had vanished. There was no VOILA! It seemed like the only French she had retained was French toast.

It did not take long for Mrs. Saint to realize that Mollie had not retained a year's worth of French. She wished she had a croissant to give Mollie for comfort.

Before she left, Mrs. Saint had sentenced Mollie to summer school. Mollie knew it was necessary. When she had been a little girl, Helen had told her, "You talk just to hear your head rattle." Now Mollie's head was rattling because it was empty with apparently one brain cell that was bouncing around.

The day after Mollie came home, Dr. Martin Luther King Jr. was assassinated. Mollie felt terrible. Mayhem ensued in different cities.

Bud felt terrible too. In March he had received another phone call and was asked for a progress report "on your plans." Bud lied and said things were right on schedule. He absolutely had nothing to do with this assassination. He was nervous about losing his two youngest children. Bud was playing with matches. More accurately he was playing with a bonfire. He began taking Helen's Librium.

Not everything was somber in the Skilss household. Since Mollie had been six years old, she had pestered her parents for a dog. They always countered with, "We need a bigger backyard."

With the purchase of their colonial they had a big backyard for the last two years. Mollie eyed it with glee.

In mid-April 1968 they brought home an eight week old black poodle from a breeder. She was named Lassie after the TV dog that the children had adored. Lassie was not a collie, but was smart and beautiful. Her registered name was La Belle Lassie Noire.

Lassie was confined to the kitchen at first like a French pastry. She cried the first night because she was away from her mother. Lassie quickly adapted to her new family. She found that they were full of unconditional love when she chewed up the wooden kitchen chairs. Becoming housebroken was a snap especially with the big back yard just waiting for Lassie.

Lassie loved to play and she was quick. When the kids were playing football, Lassie found a fumble and bit that football like a crazed linebacker. She bloodied herself and the football. With her new stitches she had something in common with the football.

Bud and Helen felt good about finally granting Mollie's wish of getting a dog. Bud and Helen did not feel good about themselves.

Bud began tossing and turning at night. Nightmares surfaced for him too. Both Helen and Bud got up at night to pace. Helen's nightmares had doubled since JFK's assassination. She was miserable enough during the day so it seemed unfair that she would be so miserable at night.

One night Bud and Helen were wide awake together. Helen broke the silence. "Some of my Librium is missing. Do you think one of the kids is taking it?"

Bud wanted to lie, but too much of his life was a lie. He wanted to be able to get some sleep at night.

"No, honey. I've been taking it. My stress level is way high."

"You have been having nightmares too, haven't you?"

"Yes, they must be contagious." Bud chuckled at what seemed humorous at three in the morning.

Helen decided to forge ahead. "I have a theory."

"Is it as good as Einstein's?"

"Maybe not." Helen was determined not to stop. "I was thinking that having nightmares comes from keeping secrets."

Bud turned warm like the milk he drank to help him sleep. "Do you have a secret?" Bud knew that by turning the tables that the furniture could be rearranged so Bud could mix things up.

"Do you have a secret?" Helen knew her husband well enough to know that he did.

Bud paused. His secrets were hideous. He would risk his marriage if he risked divulging his private demons. Bud felt like a dead duck that had been hunted down. "No," he said. Bud paused. "I have two."

"I admire your honesty," Helen said. "I have two secrets also."

"John told me that you were keeping something from me."

"He didn't tell you what?" Helen was amazed. John was a good friend.

"Did he tell you one of my secrets?" Bud was curious. It seemed John could be trusted as much as a priest who hears confession.

Helen shook her head no.

"My secrets are bizarre," said Helen. "I can't explain them."

"My secrets are hideous," said Bud. "I'm not sure how they happened."

"Do you want to tell me your secrets?"

Bud thought that was a good question. "I don't want to, but I think we need to know what is going on with each other."

Helen went first. "My one secret goes back over twenty years ago when I worked at Wright Field. One day a plane came in and it was carrying a load of space creatures." Helen described the creatures to Bud. She waited for him to laugh.

Bud gave a low whistle that turned Lassie's attention. "That's incredible."

"The weird thing is that I'm more afraid the military will take vengeance on me than I'm scared of any space aliens."

Helen filled in the other details about how she kicked the Colonel and how she disposed of the Coke® that she was sure contained some kind of drug to erase her memory.

"Now I understand your nightmares. As long as you don't go to the press about it, you should be safe from the military."

"What if aliens try to locate me to find out what I know or, worse yet, take me prisoner?"

"We have Lassie to protect you. Anyway, it's highly unlikely for that to happen after all these years."

Helen hugged Bud. "I am so glad you understand. Now what is your secret?"

Bud suddenly felt sick. It was like an instant onset of the flu.

"I'm not proud of this." Bud gulped. A golf ball feeling was blocking his throat. "My secret may sound implausible too." Bud told Helen how LBJ phoned him early in 1963. He proceeded to tell her about his trip to the ranch and LBJ's demand. When Bud said that LBJ threatened to take away Mollie if the assassination were not completed, Helen gasped. Bud talked about approaching the mob and taking care of some of the details so that JFK was assassinated.

"I didn't pull the trigger, but I might as well have."

Helen looked down at the floor. When their eyes met, their eyes were moist.

"There's something else you need to know," said Helen. Her voice was choked.

"What is that?"

"I'm JFK's sister."

Helen pummeled Bud's chest. He did not stop her. Helen fell sobbing into Bud's arms. They wordlessly held each other.

Bud broke the silence. He knew his timing was wrong, but he had to tell Helen now or never. Bud told Helen about Dr. King and how he pretended to have something to do with it so their children would not be taken away.

Helen erupted. "That's the stupidest thing I've ever heard! What were you thinking?"

"It was John's idea."

"I don't care if it were the Queen's idea."

Bud was deflated. He felt empty and confused. "I don't know what else I could have done."

Helen relented. "You were trapped. Fear is not a good place to operate from."

They held each other longer this time. There were no words between them and no secrets.

That night neither Bud nor Helen had nightmares. They couldn't because they both laid awake in the darkness all night.

CHAPTER 9

Mollie was on a vitamin regimen since she had been released from the hospital. Every day at school she had to take the numerous pills at lunch. She hid it fairly well in part because of her palming technique she had learned doing magic tricks. Her friends never asked her about it.

Mollie's next psychiatrist said it was "cruel" that she had only been put on vitamins. He advocated much stronger stuff.

This year of high school was without incident. She enjoyed being on the badminton team and won some trophies. Smashing the shuttlecock at her opponent was one of her favorite things to do. She loved the actual feathers on the birdie and marveled how it flew like a crazed robin.

Lassie and Mollie forged a bond. Every morning Helen would tell Lassie , "Go get Mollie up." Lassie would fly like a shuttlecock up the stairs, jump on the bed, and leap on Mollie. By this time Mollie had taught her to sit, stay, and roll over. The power of the Yummie treat held its spell over Lassie.

Mollie had a few friends. She had given up her quest to be popular.

Bud continued to be popular at work. He was a quick study and kept getting promoted. He often felt that he was deserving of this recognition, but chalked up his self-doubt to the secrets he held.

Helen had cut back on her Librium even though she felt as if she were carrying double the burden since Bud had confessed his secrets to her. She became more active in their church.

Mark had learned to control his megaphone mouth and made a small group of friends that did all kinds of interesting things. One of their favorite activities was to go to the local dump and dig up what they considered treasures. They filled bushel baskets with glass telephone insulators.

Like a first born Matt had racked up achievements and awards in high school. Now he was out of state at a prestigious college. Mollie missed him. Lassie didn't quite fill that void.

It was a cold, late April morning in 1968. Spring in Chicago sometimes calls out for hot chocolate. Bud was at work and had just finished his hot chocolate from the cafeteria. The heat was valiantly trying to do its job, but some of Bud's coworkers still had their coats on.

The phone rang.

Bud answered it cheerfully. "Hello."

It was that dreaded drawl. "This is the cowboy."

"So." Bud was acting brave even though he didn't feel that way."

"You are going to knock off Robert Kennedy. If you don't, all three of your children will be in danger."

Bud started to protest. "Don't bully---"

Click. The cowboy had hung up. He had lassoed his calf.

Anger bubbled up in Bud. Killing was not his hobby. He walked outside without a coat to freeze off his intense emotion. This lunacy had to stop. Bud came back inside and sipped another hot chocolate. It was his only comfort at that moment.

Bud went home that evening and told Helen about LBJ's command.

"He is mean and evil," said Helen. "He is picking you up by your ears like he picks up his beagles by their ears."

"What am I going to do?" said Bud.

"I think this calls for inviting John over for dinner."

"I'll call him in the morning."

The next morning John got Bud's call. He was hung over. People have different ways of contending with secrets.

Bud could tell that John's head wasn't clear by the way he sounded. Bud acted like everything was normal since everyone has their own pride threshold.

"Can you come over for dinner tonight? Helen is fixing the spaghetti you like so much."

John craved their company as much as their spaghetti. "I accept."

"Good. There are strings attached so don't feel like you have to bring the Fannie May® chocolates."

"I may anyway." John was generous to a San Andreas Fault. After he hung up, he worked on getting rid of his hangover. He fixed a martini even though it was before noon. The hair of the dog had to be shed.

John arrived at the Skilss's house at six o'clock. The spaghetti sauce was gurgling on the stove and its scent was permeating throughout the house. It gave John a warm welcome along with Bud's greetings. John forked over the Fannie May® candy in its white glossy box that begged people to take seconds.

Lassie greeted John and sniffed his shoes enthusiastically. Mark and Mollie appeared and said hi to this man who was like a favorite uncle. Little did they realize that he was their uncle. Bud hung up his coat.

During dinner the conversation flowed. There always seemed to be more than enough to talk about. Dessert was meringue shells with vanilla ice cream and thawed strawberries. After having their Fannie May® candies Mark and Mollie excused themselves to do homework.

John and Bud helped Helen carry the dishes from the table to the kitchen. Helen spoke to Bud.

"Why don't you apprise John of the situation? I'll be with you in a little bit."

John and Bud settled into the family room. Helen did the dishes. Then she helped herself to another Fannie Mae. She thought it would alleviate some of her tension.

Bud told John about his call from LBJ and that he had asked him to kill Robert Kennedy. John was perplexed.

"Why on earth would he call you in the first place?"

Bud could not look at John. Still not making eye contact Bud told him, "LBJ asked me to kill JFK. I made some of the arrangements."

John put his head into his hands. He rubbed his eyes. Then he cracked his knuckles.
"YOU? Of all people!"

"I felt I didn't have much choice. He threatened to take away Mollie."

"What did LBJ threaten this time?"

"All three of our kids would be in danger. I think LBJ is capable of anything."

"Why you?"

"One time he said he knew something about me."

"What?"

"I don't know."

"Should I hypnotize you?"

Bud felt that cold fear grip him. "Helen told me that you hypnotized her and that she is John and Robert's sister. I don't think that is what LBJ is hanging over my head."

"Did Helen tell you the rest of it?"

"What rest of it?"

The blue eyes met the brown eyes. "I am a Kennedy too. I am Joe Kennedy."

Bud's eyes looked pained. "There's no way I can kill Bobby or have him killed."

Helen walked into the room followed by Lassie. "Did you tell him?"

"Yes," said Bud and John simultaneously.

"There's no way I can kill another Kennedy," said Bud.

"Good to hear it," said John. He tried to lighten his tone, but it came across as sarcastic.

"Do you think our children would be harmed by LBJ?" asked Helen.

John answered. "Whoever would have thought we would be hidden away?"

Helen felt like crying. She dabbed her eyes with a tissue. She petted Lassie to comfort herself. "There's no way we can be part of killing our brother."

"Did you see Bobby on Jack Parr?" John was getting an idea.

"Yes," Helen said.

"He seemed unhappy," said John. "He didn't smile. His expression was flat."

"What are you getting at, John?" asked Bud.

"I think he would welcome a way out. He could have a life of anonymity. He could be hidden away like Helen and me."

Bud was beginning to have a glimmer of hope. "Can we do it?"

Helen said, "Mollie's magic books detail illusions that are more complicated than this would be."

John spoke next. "The details will be tricky. One thing we will have to have is a scapegoat. He will take the fall for the assassination even though it's a sham."

"Do we have the contacts and the manpower?" Bud wanted this to work.

"I have a bunch of classmates from the University of Chicago whom I saw recently at our annual reunion. They will be willing to do this I'm sure. There's nothing like bonding over martinis."

"What do you want me to do?" asked Bud.

"Get the assassin. I'll put the plan in place with him and fake an arrangement to pay him."

"Sounds dangerous."

"People will be all over him. Don't worry, Bud. We don't want to lose Bobby."

"Or our three children," said Bud.

"Let's play a game of Scrabble®," said Helen. She brought out another round of chocolates. They finished off the box.

On June 5th, 1968 Mollie Skilss read the front page of The Chicago Tribune. Robert F. Kennedy had been assassinated. She was horrified. The newspaper account said the gunman was Sirhan Sirhan. He had been a dishwasher at the local restaurant The Indian Trail where the Skilss family liked to dine on Sundays after church. Mollie's immediate thought was this was more than a coincidence. She read all the accounts and then folded up the paper to gently put it on the footstool.

Bud picked it up later and smiled. They had done it. Bobby was still alive.

Mollie did not understand the violence in the last half decade. She could not articulate her thoughts. The Skilss family did not talk at all about what happened. It was as if it were not talked about then it did not exist.

A year later Mollie finished her junior year of high school. She knew her extra poundage would not earn her a badge of popularity. She had given up her dream of becoming a cheerleader and was content with being in the small circle of friends that she did have. They were good enough friends that no one asked Mollie what had happened or where she had been when she was hospitalized.

Mollie had her first date that year. She maintained good grades. She kept taking all of those nuisance vitamins.

It was the early summer of 1969. Within days of the first anniversary of Bobby Kennedy's murder, Mollie woke up screaming in the middle of the night. She wound up being psychiatrically hospitalized for the second time.

She ended up in a suburban hospital's psychiatric unit. Darren happened to be there too. Mollie was put in a room with an older woman who looked like a ghost. The woman stayed in bed all day. At night when Mollie was trying to sleep, this poltergeist figure would go over to Mollie's bed and just stare at her. Mollie kept her eyes half shut and wished the woman would go away.

Mollie had a new psychiatrist whom she couldn't stand. She gave him the silent treatment which is not the brightest tactic to use on a psychiatrist since their whole craft is based on verbalizations.

This pudgy piece of ego pressured her to sign a consent so she would be given electric convulsive treatment otherwise known as ECT. Mollie resisted until she gave up one day out of anger and gave her permission, It was like she was being returned to the pumpkin patch.

Mollie was not sure where her anger was coming from, but she directed it in a passive way. When her parents visited, she played the Nancy Sinatra record and sang along with it. "These boots were made for walking and that's what they'll do. They'll walk all over you."

Mollie was not out of it enough to miss the moon walk. She and Darren were given special permission to stay up and watch the astronauts land on the moon and then take the first steps on its surface. Mollie was awed. To think that years later that people thought it was faked. They had the wrong event.

CHAPTER 10

By the fall of 1969 Mollie was on some heavy duty medication. Not only was she taking Thorazine®, but she had been diagnosed as schizophrenic. She went to see Dr. Pudgy once a week. Mollie sat like a lump while he asked her what her grades were. He spent most of the sessions trying to light his pipe. If his success at lighting his pipe indicated how good of a psychiatrist he was, he was a miserable failure as a shrink. He had a model of the brain on his desk which Mollie did not think went well with the decor.

For some reason Dr. Pudgy recommended that Mollie take dancing lessons. Mollie much preferred her horseback riding lessons that she took as a sophomore in high school.

She took a battery of psychology tests and was told that she was smart. Mollie thought she was smarter than the I.Q. test indicated, but she kept her mouth shut like she did for all of her sessions.

Mollie decided that she wanted to go to a college close by home. She found one that was forty-five minutes away. The campus was treelined with a large grassy area called The Mall in front of the Student Union. The Mall stretched to the Chapel. There was a clock beneath the Chapel spire. During homecoming one year someone had painted Mickey Mouse on it with his white gloved hands pointing to the time.

Classroom buildings and dorms lined the perimeter of the Mall. It was a small, but attractive campus. There were approximately 1,200 students here which was about the size of her high school. Mollie wasn't so concerned anymore about how popular she would be here, but how well she would fit in. She looked at the Chapel clock. Time would tell.

Mollie's senior year went without incident before she went off to college. She took easier classes including Home Economics. It turned out to be a challenging experience when they were making meringue shells in Home Ec. The class was instructed to add the sugar gradually into the mixing bowl. Mollie's classmates took the sugar bag and Mollie reminded them to add the ingredient slowly. Whoosh! The sugar was dumped in all at once. Mollie knew the ramifications which meant tough meringue to play havoc with molars. This was the start of a trend that Mollie began to notice over the years which was, "No one ever listens to me."

That was the most traumatic thing that happened to Mollie in her senior year. She liked her speed reading class. Every night Mollie was free to watch TV since she had finished her homework at school. She watched Bewitched and Laugh In as well as Lost In Space.

Meanwhile, Bud had been promoted to Vice-President of his company. He flourished in this leadership role. He wondered sometimes if his roles with King and the Kennedys were behind his advancement. He did not know it, but they had nothing to do with it.

Helen was happier. She was pleased with the extra money coming into the house. Their financial obligation to the mob had been met.

Helen was faced with Mollie being taken away from her during Mollie's last hospitalization. Dr. Pudgy asked Mollie if she would like to be put in a foster family. Mollie had answered with a resounding no. Mollie didn't think Dr. Pudgy had her best interests at heart. She didn't want to be away from her family.

Dr. Pudgy was so expressionless and lacked any warmth unless it was coming from the bowl of his pipe. It was no surprise to Mollie when she read in the paper years later that this psychiatrist had switched his practice to acupuncture.

Helen and Bud loaded up Mollie's things (and her Thorazine®) and took her to college in the fall of 1970. Goodbyes are difficult at this juncture. One is not just saying goodbye because of dropping someone off for a stay. It is more primal than that. It is a rite of passage where the goodbye is saying so long to the way a relationship has been. It is goodbye to how things are right now.

Mollie and Helen choked up as they hugged. Helen hoped Mollie could handle college. Mollie hoped her mother could handle her rapidly emptying nest.

Mollie met her roommate Darlene who prided herself on being the studious type. Darlene was so very serious and eventually that led to their falling out with each other.

Towards the end of the first semester Darlene pulled the window blind down and it promptly fell on the floor. Mollie rolled over in laughing hysterics. It had looked like slapstick. Darlene scoffed and said, "In my family that wouldn't be funny at all." Mollie was stuck with a wet blanket which would never dry out.

Another incident occurred around Mollie's preparation for speech class. The assignment was to make a speech and demonstrate something while doing this. Mollie chose to talk about Houdini and to use his catch phrase, "Will wonders never cease?" Using a magic trick as the demonstration for her speech she practiced in front of Darlene.

The trick involved showing an empty glass, putting a tube over it, and pouring water from a clear pitcher into the glass. When the tube was removed, the glass was filled with colored water. When Mollie did the trick for Darlene, the water turned a bright yellow. To add to the effect Mollie said, "Will wonders never cease?" and chugged the water.

Darlene exclaimed in disgust, "Oh, yuck!"

Being suggestible, Mollie immediately vomited. Darlene ran to the women's restroom to get paper towels, but was out of luck because there were only hand dryers.

Darlene moved out at the start of the second semester. Neither one of them grieved.

Mollie pledged a sorority and enjoyed all of the shenanigans. One night the pledges were taken to O'Hare Airport where they played relay races in the middle of the terminal. They were kicked out of the airport, but they had gotten in quite a few games.

They went snipe hunting in the local cemetery with their pillowcases ready to trap the snipes. Unfortunately there were no snipes to be found.

Mollie decided to play a joke on the regular members of the sorority. Four members shared a dorm room. Mollie took an envelope and filled it with shaving cream. Then she wedged the envelope under the sorority sisters' door and stomped on the envelope. The idea was that the shaving cream would go flying across their floor.

What Mollie had not anticipated was that there was no exit for her without being seen. Several nights later she returned to her dorm room and it was a disaster area. There was shaving cream in her shoes and thread was strung taut at all levels of height in her room. It took her a long time to do the cleanup and to thread her way through the maze with scissors.

The pledges had an overnight at another pledge's house. They finished making their paddles. They were already changed into their pajamas when they decided to go out for a doughnut run. It was about one in the morning. They had purchased their doughnuts from the drive through and were on their way back to the house. Suddenly a police siren was on top of them. Apparently they had not seen the red light. Mild hysteria prevailed in the car.

The one pledge fortunately had a brother on the local police force. Once that was established, the car full of pledges, pajamas, and doughnuts were let go. The scent of the doughnuts may have interfered with the cop's judgment.

This is how the first two years of Mollie's college proceeded. She was far from serious.

Mollie decided her major during her sophomore year. It was not a rational decision. Her friend mentioned that she was going to a tea at the Speech Pathology and Audiology Department. Mollie went along and liked the hors d'oeuvres. She also liked the clinic and the hearing test equipment. Her first course had to do with phonetics and she did not exactly gravitate to it.

For her junior year there was a young professor Dr. Bangood who joined the department. Mollie liked her dry wit and the fact that she wore her hair in bangs like Mollie did. Dr. Bangood's enunciation was a crisp role model. Dr. Bangood did not waste time being diplomatic.

One time Mollie was arguing her point that a period needed to be within parentheses. Dr. Bangood snapped back, "If you want to look ignorant, do it that way."

Mollie liked her psychology classes. From her readings she determined she was most likely a manic depressive and not a schizophrenic. She wondered about it. No one listened to her anyway.

Mollie had a favorite joke about a class that supposedly happened. That must have meant it was apocryphal. A student studied hours on end for his biology exam. On the day of the exam he went to the huge lecture hall where he and a hundred other students were in the class. On lab tables were birds with sacks over their heads. Only their legs and feet were visible. The professor explained that the test consisted of identifying the birds by just looking at their exposed legs and feet.

The student who studied so diligently got up and said, "That's the stupidest thing I've ever heard." He went towards the door to leave.

The professor stopped him by saying, "Young man, what is your name?"

The student pulled up his jeans and said, "You tell me."

Mollie had only gotten through biology by the grace of her fellow students. They mercifully dissected the frog and the earthworm for her.

Halfway through her sophomore year Mollie quit taking her medication. She felt so much better physically after that.

On weekends Mollie frequently went home. Sometimes the majority of the activities on campus were pot smoking parties. Mollie didn't think these had any redeeming value so going home was a real treat. She drove around her parent's 1970 Mustang convertible and spent Saturday nights watching Lawrence Welk and Mary Tyler Moore on TV. Lassie jumped up on her bed as her alarm in the morning which Mollie missed in the dorm.

Mollie's senior year became more eventful. One day she visited a friend of hers in the dorm. Mollie spontaneously flopped face down on the spare bed and cried out, "Why did they have to kill Bobby Kennedy?"

She had no idea where that came from. She began having trouble sleeping. Mollie felt like a wreck.

Going over to Dr. Bangood's house seemed like a good idea. Her husband greeted Mollie at the door and invited her in. Dr. Bangood urged her to sit on the sofa.

Mollie talked for hours while Dr. Bangood rocked in her rocking chair. Some might say that was symbolic i.e. Mollie being off her rocker. Dr. Bangood fixed tea and they sipped the afternoon away. Mollie told Dr. Bangood about her psychiatric history.

They talked about whether it would be a good idea for Mollie to see her psychiatrist whom Mollie had stopped seeing for a year and a half. Mollie allowed that she probably should, but wasn't wild about the idea.

Dr. Bangood called a colleague from the Speech Pathology Department who came over and took over. That colleague made calls from the other room and informed Mollie that Dr. Pudgy was on vacation. Mollie was secretly pleased. An appointment was made for that night with a psychiatrist in Wilmette which was close to where Mollie lived. The colleague, Dr. Bangood, and Mollie loaded up into the car and took off for what Mollie hoped was not another psychiatric hospitalization.

They went to the psychiatrist's home which had a back entrance and a second story office over the garage. The psychiatrist was a woman whom Mollie thought was intriguing and was most likely a good sign after having two previous male doctors. Mollie was at the bottom of the stairwell when Dr. Marjorie Minton emerged at the top of the stairs. Mollie immediately liked her November appropriate red sweater vest. She carried it off well with her jet black hair. Dr. Minton was trim and looked to be about forty years old.

Mollie was escorted into her office which was the size of a medium bedroom. Mollie was glad there was no analyst's couch, no model of the brain, and no tamping of a pipe. Instead, there was a sofa that Mollie sat on and a chair perpendicular to that. Dr. Minton sat in the chair. This would be their seating arrangement for the next nineteen years.

Mollie lapsed at first into the silence she had not enjoyed with Dr. Pudgy. Then all she did was talk about her grades. After about ten years Dr. Minton told Mollie how "boring" these first sessions were.

Mollie was immature. She did not mature until she turned fifty.

The week leading up to Mollie's college graduation tapped into her enthusiasm. Because of her excitement she could not sleep. She stayed up all night for three nights in a row. Mollie greeted the dawns by toasting them with apricot juice. Her parents were out of town and had dropped off the Mustang for her to use.

Mollie noticed helicopters hovering over the campus. She believed there were more strangers on campus. She began to panic. She called Dr. Minton who agreed to see her that evening. Mollie had no money so she sailed through the toll booths without paying. Her driving made a student driver look like a pro.

She reached Dr. Minton's house after dark. She could barely stay awake. In fact, she dozed off several times as Dr. Minton was talking to her.

Dr. Minton and her husband (also a psychiatrist) drove Mollie to psychiatric hospitalization number three. They stopped for ice cream along the way which helped sweeten the sting.

CHAPTER 11

Mollie missed her college graduation ceremony. However, she was not allowed to miss her doses of Thorazine® in the hospital. Once the male nurse put the medication into orange juice which infuriated Mollie for no good psychotic reason. She kicked him in the groin and she ended up in restraints.

Mollie shared a room with someone who looked like Patty Hearst. Who would believe her if she were? Mollie would just be regarded as crazy. So one afternoon in a delusional sprint, Mollie ran down the hall yelling, "I'm Patty Hearst I'm Patty Hearst." No one paid any attention to her, so she surmised that the staff knew who was the real Patty Hearst.

Shortly after this, Mollie's roommate was moved. By the time Mollie was discharged, she knew she wasn't Patty Hearst, but she wasn't sure about the other patient. The other patient would sit next to a patient who looked like the singer Mama Cass. They would peruse the newspaper and the Patty patient would ask the Mama Cass patient, "What does that mean?" It was as if they thought the newspaper were written in some kind of code. The hospital was a Federal Mental Health Center so it wasn't beyond the realm of possibility that Patty Hearst was there.

Patty was discharged in the company of another patient. The other patient left carrying a suitcase of soda pop. She ordered extra sodas at meals. Mollie could hear the clank of the cans as the woman carried them out.

A couple of years later Mollie was looking at Helen's Good Housekeeping magazine. There was a photograph of Patty Hearst with a female identified as one of her bodyguards. Patty Hearst looked just like the patient who had been Mollie's hospital roommate. The bodyguard looked exactly like the soda can lugging patient. As Houdini would say, "Will wonders never cease?"

Mollie was discharged soon enough to enroll in the fall semester at Western Michigan University. She had been accepted there for their renowned graduate program in Speech Pathology.

Mollie had struggled with coming to terms with what she wanted to do with her life. This was shown even when she slept. When she roomed with Darlene in college, Darlene told her of an incident when Darlene returned to the room one night. Mollie was in bed fast asleep. Darlene opened the door to enter and Mollie sat bold upright in bed.

"What do you want to be?" she asked Darlene.

"A librarian," said Darlene.

"No, what do you want to BE?"

"A butterfly," answered Darlene.

With that Mollie laid back down and continued her sweet dreams.

At Western Michigan Mollie grew even more unsure about what she wanted to be. Being a butterfly sounded fairly good at this point.

She struggled with the lengthy spectrographs known as voice prints in lay terms. These were unwieldy at over six feet in length. They had to be ironed. This called for taking better care of these pieces of paper than she took care of her clothes.

Mollie's roommate at Western Michigan was pursuing a graduate degree in psychology which Mollie thought was probably a more interesting choice for herself. Her roommate's father had been a Secret Service Agent assigned to President Kennedy.

The one redeeming factor for Mollie's time at Western Michigan was playing on the coed touch football team. It was the first time she had ever been on artificial turf. She was disappointed to be assigned the position of center. In her family's backyard touch football games she had been an awesome wide receiver.

Mollie knew she could not keep up with her homework load and with ironing the voice prints. The Thorazine® was slowing her down. She decided to drop out after a month and a half. She knew her parents would not be happy about this decision and she was right.

Mollie came home and felt defeated as much as she felt lost. She spent time retreated to her room. Helen and Bud expected her to get a job.

The only thing worse than hunting for a job is getting rejected for a job. Mollie was unable to find anything even though she made a major effort to break through her medication haze. It looked bleak.

Thanksgiving was a week away and Mollie still had not found a job. Bud and Helen went out one night and Mollie decided she had enough. She downed a bunch of Thorazine® which were not that easy to swallow. Then Mollie put a short suicide note on Helen's desk and went to bed.

It seemed like a short time later that she heard her mother's panicked voice yell, "BUD!"

Mollie was pulled out of bed and taken to the bathroom where Helen poured mustard water down

Mollie's throat. This was the same way that vomiting was induced in Lassie when she ate the chocolates under the Christmas tree.

Thorazine® is a bulky pill and the pills started going up Mollie's nose. It was an uncomfortable feeling like burning M & M's.® Having her stomach pumped would have been an even more uncomfortable feeling.

The next morning Dr. Minton saw Mollie along with Bud and Helen. Mollie was hospitalized for a couple of days. She just kept repeating how stupid it was for her to try and kill herself.

After being released from the hospital, Mollie found a job at a department store in the toy department. She adored this job except for one aspect. Christmas was approaching and Mollie was expected to gift wrap toys for the customers who requested this service.

Mollie's fine motor coordination ranked up there with her ironing skills. She noticed that she would clumsily wrap a gift for a customer and then the next customer in line would say, "You don't need to wrap mine. Just give me the paper and ribbon and I will do it myself."

There were two particularly challenging toys that took Mollie forever to wrap. Neither one was in a box. One of these was a ventriloquist dummy and the other was a basketball. Wrapping these tied up Mollie for some time.

Mollie was bothered that she did not have direction for her life. She rationalized it by telling herself she was young and still had her whole life in front of her.

After Christmas she found a slightly better paying job at an insurance company. All day long she stood and filed. There was a brief one hour respite where she sorted and distributed the mail throughout the office. The other employees acted as if she were invisible and visions of junior high school popped up into Mollie's head.

One night she composed a humorous newsletter and put one on everyone's desk before they came in. It caused a flurry of excitement. Since Mollie had written it anonymously, there was speculation about who could have done such a masterpiece. No one suspected Mollie.

Finally a reward was posted. If the perpetrator came forward with the original, that person would be treated to a free lunch. Mollie held out overnight, but confessed the following day. Everyone took her out and it was the most festive burger Mollie had ever had. It was the beginning of Mollie no longer being a pariah.

Eight months later Mollie had her application in at Northwestern University for a graduate degree in Guidance Counseling. She had also interviewed for a position doing layouts at a downtown sewage magazine. Mollie had done layouts for her college yearbook. She had also applied to a group therapist training program at Woods Hospital, a private psychiatric hospital in suburban Chicago.

The sewage magazine Waste Away offered Mollie a position in the mailroom. Mollie had enough of mailrooms for the last eight months. Northwestern University accepted her into their program. Woods Hospital accepted Mollie for their group therapist training. Mollie decided to go through Woods Hospital's training.

Mollie liked the setting for Woods Hospital. It was by a river that was shaded by trees. One time she noticed a sign nailed to one of the trees by the river that read, "DO NOT FEED THE DOLPHINS."

The back part of the property was heavily wooded. This is where weekend cookouts were held. The hospital building was unimaginative. There were no bars over the windows with the unspoken assumption that things were so good there that no one would want to escape. It was a small place. It housed no more than one hundred patients.

Each unit had a dayroom with comfortable sofas, chairs and a coffee table. There was a separate TV room for each unit. Coffee was readily available and smoking was allowed. It looked like there was a permanent rain cloud in the hallway from the cigarette haze. As one employee told Mollie, "If you don't smoke now, you will start."

The dining room was light and smoke free. It was cafeteria style. One time the menu choice was either meatballs or chicken breasts. The server bellowed out, "BOOBS OR BALLS?"

The actual group therapist training was not something that came naturally to Mollie. It would take her another twenty years to become proficient.

The class spent all day sitting on the floor. They had renowned speakers like James Masterson who was THE authority on borderline personality disorder. The widow of Rolf who developed the Rolfing technique also lectured. Sufis came and danced around. Staff psychiatrists came and gave talks. Psychology came alive for Mollie and she loved it even though she wasn't the most skilled group therapist.

Playing different group therapy types of games was a favorite part of the training for Mollie. There was one which was one that Mollie really liked. Everybody stretched face up on the floor. One person put their head on top of another's stomach. Then a person would put their head on that person's tummy. There would be a whole line of people with a head on another's stomach. They were connected like parallel and perpendicular sardines. Then the first person in the line would say, 'HO HO HO" and keep repeating it while everyone down the line did it too. It did not take long for everyone to erupt in laughter as heads bounced up and down on tummies. No wonder the name of the game was "Chuckle Belly."

Then the class was divided into four groups. Twice a week for a long afternoon these groups met to practice group therapy. One person was selected to be the therapist and everyone else had to be a group member. A trainer sat and observed.

Mollie was more skilled as a patient than as a group therapist. In one practice group she confessed her psychiatric history. She began to notice the glazed look that came into people's eyes when she talked about this. It was a look that was a mix of pity, horror, and disappointment.

At the end of every week the group did a sociogram of how each member did as a therapist. Each group member ranked the others in order of their proficiency. With one exception Mollie was always ranked last. She knew she was bad, but not the worst. She attributed her poor showing to her confession. The others were seeing her in a more negative light. That's what she told herself so she would not go without sleep for three days and three nights.

Other than this Mollie felt accepted by the group. They laughed at her humor and they teased her. Helen had always told Mollie that people only teased the ones they liked.

Mollie thought the others played it safe in group therapy. They did not disclose much of significance. It dawned on Mollie later that either they were holding out or they had led miserably uninteresting lives.

Mollie continued her "real" therapy with Dr. Minton. She felt increasingly comfortable with the M.D. The transference was building nicely. Transference is not what you need to change buses. It is the bond that patients build with their therapist. Sometimes it mirrors a past relationship like with a parent. Mollie found that she was beginning to open up more with her.

Mollie finished her group therapist training and was hired by Woods Hospital as a mental health technician. Her poor performance in the program was validated. She was assigned to the graveyard shift. At least she didn't have to stand on her feet all day doing filing.

However, there were no groups to do therapy with from midnight to eight A.M. This way she did not run the risk of ruining anyone's psyche. Her psyche felt bruised though. Mollie had gone through three months of training to end up fighting sleep every night. Little did she know it would only get worse.

CHAPTER 12

Mollie enrolled in a university that came to the hospital to give its classes. It was reasonable and convenient. It was more of a self-learning style which meant the professors did not lecture much, but gave the students various projects to do. This was time consuming since Mollie was also working full-time at nights.

She felt like she worked in a cave. The lights were dimmed at night to provide an atmosphere of rest for the patients. Because of their medication most patients were in bed by the time Mollie started her shift.

As luck would have it, a really cute guy started working with her after a few months. Derek had blonde hair and belonged more on a surf board than in a psychiatric dayroom. He had just finished college and was figuring out what he wanted to do with his life too. Mollie found out that he had been engaged, but his fiancee had broken it off. He was traumatized by this rejection and did not want Mollie to help him through it. Mollie was very attracted to him, but he clearly regarded her as in the friend category.

They did have fun together. First, they played games at night to pass the time. Then they went horseback riding. They found a stable in McHenry, Illinois that was in the country. In the fall it was apple selling territory.

The stable had high beam rafters with gobs of gossamer spider webs spun intricately over the entire ceiling. It was a work of farm art.

The grounds were equally as beautiful. Green trees of progressive hues lined the horse trails. These led into thicker woods with old trees weighted down with age.

There was also a clearing with a shimmering lake. One could almost hear the fish sing.

One time when Derek and Mollie went riding, they dismounted by the lake to rest. Once they mounted their horses again, the horses took off at breakneck and breathtaking speed. The horses would not respond to any command to slow down or go whoa. Derek and Mollie barely managed to hang on. Apparently the horses knew that they were close to the barn and nothing was going to stop them from their anticipated feed.

Another time Derek and Mollie went inner tubing. This was also at a farm with a steep hill. In the winter it was covered with snow and ice. A pulley hoisted each person on a sizable truck inner tube to the top of the hill. Then the person laid down on the inner tube and glided down the hill. It was a great way to bond over hot chocolate afterwards.

Mollie wished that Derek would recognize how right she was for him. He even escorted her to a wedding, but everything remained purely platonic.

In the romance department Mollie had lackluster results. She dated a guy in high school who barely spoke and when he did, he had a slight speech impediment. They kissed once, but it was so quick that it didn't count.

In college she barely dated. She had never had a long term relationship. In high school she remembered sitting on her bed and crying. Helen would come in and try to comfort her. Mollie sobbed about how she would never get married. It was a fear and an eventual truth. Helen was able to jolly Mollie out of her misery so that Mollie was able to laugh about it. Even Lassie would join them and add her four paws to comfort Mollie.

Meanwhile, Mollie enjoyed Derek's company. She hoped over time that she would grow on him. He was not partial to human fungus, so that didn't happen.

Mollie threw herself into her schoolwork. She was doing a research project which was supposed to be a group effort with three other students, but Mollie was carrying the brunt. The deadline was fast approaching and Mollie needed more time to complete what was needed. She decided to ask for some time off. Three days were all that was required.

Mollie's supervisor did not think it was as good of an idea that Mollie thought it was. She did not approve the request.

Being aware of her capabilities Mollie knew her deadline was out of reach. She was worried. She was wide awake in her bed at night. Drifting into sleep was not an option. Her eyes were popped open like she was in terror. An energy like electricity jolted through her body. It made her and the bed tremble. There was an intensity of excitement that was building in her. She was energized. She could do anything.

The next morning was a blur. She drove her car to her junior high school a couple of blocks away. Mollie wanted to look at a framed quote in the foyer by JFK: "Ask not what your country can do for you, but what you can do for your country." It was autographed by Kennedy. Mollie scrutinized how "John" was signed. It was exactly the way John Kendricks signed his first name. Mollie did not know what to make of this. It was odd and the day was going to get odder.

Mollie went out to her car to leave. Her car would not start. It was only four years old. She adored her car. It was a 1973 blood orange Karmann Ghia convertible.

Towards the end of its life it would eject a stream of blood orange fluid on Mollie's foot whenever she stepped on the clutch. Mollie named her car O.J. It did not have heat in the winter, but spewed out heat in the summer. It was not a reliable car which added to the thrill of driving it.

O.J. developed a rust problem later in its life. Bud did the body work on it. He used gallon after gallon of Bondo® to patch it up. He stuffed newspapers and rags in the headlight area for the Bondo® to attach itself. The headlight subsequently burned out and needed replacing. Mollie took O.J. to the shop where to her embarrassment the mechanic opened up the headlight and began pulling one long rag after another out. It was like a comedy scene.

When O.J. didn't start, Mollie's sense of agitation grew. She walked home and got into some sort of argument with Helen. She asked for the car keys to Helen's car and was refused. Mollie felt trapped. She flew out of the front door. All she wanted to do was to get away. She had called Dr. Minton earlier, but her answering service said she was out of town. Mollie did not believe this. She had to get to her. Without transportation this was going to be difficult.

As luck would have it, a neighbor teenager was driving up the street. Mollie had babysat for her when the girl had been a kid. Mollie flagged her down.

Mollie asked to be dropped off about a mile down the street as the neighbor was going to continue on in the opposite direction. Uncharacteristic for this village there was a rundown little apartment on the corner where Mollie was let out. It was across from the Police Department. On the apartment's doorway stoop was a woman doing a crossword puzzle. Mollie noticed a VW™ bug parked in the driveway. She approached the woman.

"Can you give me a lift?"

"What?"

"Can you give me a ride?"

"My husband will be back any minute and he can give you a ride."

Mollie showed the most patience she had all day even though it amounted to about three minutes. Then a man rounded the corner. He was black and bigger than 200 pounds. In front of him on two leashes were two Doberman Pinschers.

Feeling intimidated, Mollie wanted to back out, but didn't want to look prejudiced. The guy's wife explained Mollie's request. The guy happily agreed. Mollie continued to be at unease.

For the last two months a black man had raped two women in the area. He was known as "The Evanston Rapist." This rapist would take his victims to a park near Northwestern University and sexually assault them.

For no good reason Mollie's gut instinct told her this guy was The Evanston Rapist. She would have to be careful.

The guy and Mollie got into the car. It was a paler orange than her Karmann Ghia and probably an older model. It certainly was running better than hers.

Wordlessly the guy pulled into a liquor store on Green Bay Road. Mollie told him she would wait in the car! After he went into the store, Mollie gave a fleeting thought to fleeing. She feared him enough to want to escape, but feared him enough to not try and escape. Mollie was stuck between the devil and the pale orange car.

The guy eventually emerged from the liquor store like he was victoriously holding trophies. He had a bottle of wine and two plastic champagne glasses. Mollie did not see anything to celebrate here. All she wanted was a ride. Pepsi® would have been so much more welcome than the wine.

Mollie learned the guy's name was Richard. He was affable and talkative. Mollie gave him directions to Dr. Minton's house. Finally they arrived at her home. Mollie rang the doorbell and no one was home just like the answering service had said. All of a sudden the most bizarre thing happened.

A helicopter zoomed down and hovered just above where Mollie was standing in the driveway. The side door of the helicopter was open and Mollie could see a man in Army fatigues and hat. Mollie ran over to the garage and plastered herself against the door. She was petrified. Richard came from around the side of the house like everything was normal. Maybe Mollie needed some wine after all.

Richard drove Mollie to a park near Northwestern University. Mollie had a sinking feeling which validated her gut feeling. Richard spread a blanket on the grass and proceeded to open the bottle of wine. He poured two glasses of wine for them.

Mollie told Richard that she did not want to be locked up and outlined a little bit of her psychiatric history. Then she switched her plan. She decided to keep this guy talking. He talked a lot. Several times he reached for the wine bottle, but Mollie made sure she took hold of it first to pour him a drink. She was afraid he was going to smash the bottle over her head.

At one point Richard said he had taught poetry. Mollie's immediate internal reaction was that he had probably done this in prison. She had him recite something he had written. It was better than the wine.

Mollie said she was ready to leave. They packed up the car and Richard drove to his place. Mollie went inside and Richard went to another room to talk with his wife. Mollie's fear gauge kicked in again. She sat in the living room in a semi-frozen state. If she were going to bolt, she had better do it now. She burst through the front door and sprinted faster than when she qualified for the Junior Olympics as a ten year old. Mollie ran across the street to the Police Station.

She wanted to tell the Police that she knew where the Evanston rapist was. Unfortunately she had no proof and didn't want to be regarded as crazy. Instead, she asked the Police to call her father to pick her up.

As bad luck would have it, her father and Richard arrived at the same time. How Richard tracked her down she would never know. Richard and her father exchanged handshakes and Richard took her father off to the side. Mollie was afraid he was telling her father that she needed to be locked up. She wanted to scream. Then she heard her father telling Richard where they lived. This did not feel right at all.

It was dark out by now and Mollie's mood had gone from ecstatic earlier in the day to a more dark mood. She was hungry and tired. She had not had any lunch or dinner. The little bit of wine she had was curdling her mouth.

Once at home Mollie and her parents began to argue. She felt like she had to flee again. She went to the back door to run and Helen was there. She slapped Mollie across the face.

Mollie ran into the kitchen and dialed 9-1-1. She already had a call in to Dr. Minton's answering service. After Mollie called 9-1-1, Bud used a wrestling hold to pin Mollie to the floor.

The answering service called and talked to Bud as he held Mollie down. When he hung up, he was crying. "They want to take her to London."

Mollie cleared up the confusion. "That's a hospital in Chicago. It's called London Memorial (later its name was changed). Mollie always wondered why her father thought it was plausible that she should be taken out of the country for treatment.

An ambulance arrived along with the Police. Mollie requested transport to the hospital where Dr. Minton had her hospitalized before this. She sat up front with the paramedics and even operated the siren once.

Mollie spent a month in the hospital. She was able to write one of her papers for her Master's degree while hospitalized.

A most unusual thing happened to her while she was staring out of her window one afternoon. A flying silver disc that looked like a hamburger in a bun was floating over the Chicago skyline. At that moment Dr. Minton showed up at the door and Mollie said she wanted to show her something (the flying object).

"Just a minute," said Dr. Minton and she left. The window of opportunity was gone. It was not a hallucination because the only time Mollie had a visual hallucination was before her first hospitalization as a teenager.

After her release from the hospital, Mollie and her parents went out for a Hackneyburger near where they lived. They broke the news to Mollie that Richard was the Evanston rapist.

Mollie cried because she had already sensed that. He had been arrested. He had raped at least one woman after Mollie had spent time with him.

Helen noted that he had not raped Mollie. "It's probably the nicest thing he has ever done."

Mollie decided to hang out at the library. She stumbled across some books about UFOs. One book detailed an October, 1962 UFO sighting by a policeman in Ravenna, Ohio.

Ravenna was the town next to Kent where Mollie had lived. The policeman chased the UFO all the way into Pennsylvania until he ran out of gas. This occurred a little more than two months after the Skilss moved from Kent to the Chicago area. Mollie wondered if the UFO were looking for her.

Mollie returned to work and was ostracized. One day in the tiny conference room one of the female staff members was crying. Other staff members were hovering over her. Mollie went into the room and was ready to offer some comforting words when the crying woman pointed her finger at Mollie and announced, "I don't want her in here."

It was a mystery to Mollie where this irrational dislike came from. She left the room and left part of her self-esteem behind. The Evanston rapist liked her. Why didn't normal people?

CHAPTER 13

One day Mollie was hunkered over the nursing station doing her charting. A new mental health technician came up to her and said, "I'd like to be your friend."

Mollie looked up. She saw Judy who was blonde haired, blue-eyed, and had missed her calling as a model. Mollie wondered many times what possessed Judy to approach her like that. Judy was everything that Mollie was not. She was sexy, gregarious and lived on drinking diet sodas and smoking cigarettes. Judy was newly divorced.

Knowing how rejection is a Muhammad Ali phenomenon ("It floats like a butterfly and stings like a bee") Mollie accepted Judy's offer of friendship. They began to get to know each other.

Judy said she was a "dog" person. She had raised a number of English Sheep Dogs. Helen pointed out to Mollie how Lassie was not enamored with Judy when she came over to visit.

Mollie often stayed overnight on the sofa at Judy's apartment. They would sit on the balcony and talk while Judy smoked. Judy fancied herself as the rebel of her family. She told Mollie how she broke the news to her Methodist mother that she drank and smoked. The way she did it was to invite her mother to lunch and then Judy lit up her cigarette after ordering a drink.

Mollie couldn't imagine being a smoker or drinker much less doing this to Helen. Mollie wasn't sure what Judy's investment was in smoking. It was a plain old addiction.

Of course, that addiction along with Judy's penchant for diet cola kept her at 92 pounds. Those vices arguably had their payoff.

Judy and Mollie had fun together. It was a sisterly as well as a friend bond. One time by the pool Judy noticed that Mollie's second toe was longer than her big toe.

Judy made her proclamation. "That means you are closely related to monkeys."

"No, it means I am descended from royalty." Mollie had actually read that in The Chicago Tribune.

Another time Judy and Mollie went grocery shopping in the winter. Judy randomly tossed items into her grocery cart. Mollie had never seen anyone shop without looking at the prices. Outside, as Judy pushed the cart to her car, she fell on her butt. Perhaps if he had a longer second toe, she could have steadied herself.

Mollie taught Judy how to play backgammon which was the pastime of the late seventies. They were well matched, but Mollie usually edged her out. Over backgammon they talked about many things.

One thing came out of nowhere which Mollie wondered about. Mollie's father had been on the Board of Directors of a national publishing company after climbing the ranks. Then he was suddenly fired. He found a new job at Rand McNally.

On this afternoon over a game of backgammon Judy stated, "I hate to tell you this, but your father works for the Rand Group."

"No, he works for Rand McNally," said Mollie. She could not have been more definite.

In graduate school Mollie learned later that the Rand Group was a powerful think tank. What possessed Judy to bring this up? Why did she really want to be her friend? After all, Judy was associating with someone whom she believed was closely related to monkeys.

At work Mollie and Judy were assigned to a Family Therapy Team under the leadership of a German psychiatrist Dr. Wontherr. They were assigned to the day shift. Mollie was glad her dark days were over on the graveyard shift.

Mollie and Judy got busy and taught backgammon to as many patients as they could. They perfected their strategy so as to become more competitive with each other.

They led group therapy. Mollie was pleased when one handsome patient in his thirties said, "I like the groups that Mollie does."

One day another mental health tech cornered Mollie. He asked what Mollie thought was a strange question and one that was not any of his business. "Why are you friends with Judy? You have nothing in common."

Mollie did not give an answer. What she wanted to say was that they were both Methodist, bright, keen backgammon players, dog lovers and had a good time together.

The Family Therapy Team did research after a year to see the results of treatment. Once the results were compiled, all the former patients and their families were invited back to the hospital for a celebration. This happened to fall on Mollie's birthday April Fool's Day.

Before Mollie was born Helen had kept saying, "I'm going to have an April Fool's baby." She fulfilled her prediction.

The story was that Mollie was named for "the little girl down the street that you and Matt played with." Mollie was perplexed by this. Neither she nor Matt were old enough for this and Mollie would have been born after this fact.

The truth was that Bud had been programmed to name his daughter Mollie if he had a daughter. Her name was a puzzle that she figured out years later.

Mollie joked about her birthday. As she misquoted P.T. Barnum, "A sucker is born every minute and I was born licking the lollipop."

Besides her work and her time with Judy Mollie kept busy taking Adult Enrichment Classes. She took watercolor painting and ended up with soggy paper and a fortune invested in materials. Her Creative Writing Class was fun and she met a man who was promising. He gave Mollie a copy of his published book and paid a lot of attention to her. Then one evening the wise teacher asked him how his wife was. Mollie was licking the lollipop.

Mollie took an innovative class about making artwork out of photocopies. She took in photos of Helen holding Mollie up in the air when Mollie was a baby. A man noticed these photos and incredulously commented, "Isn't that.....?" and his voice trailed off. Mollie didn't know what to make about this unfinished observation.

Mollie had a need for stimulation. Growing restless at work she was questioning what was next for her. She asked herself what many people only consider a rhetorical question. That was, "What is something I've always wanted to do?"

Maybe it had to do with the horseback riding she had done or maybe it was her penchant for westerns that led to her answer. Mollie decided she wanted to work on a dude ranch.

Mollie wasn't sure where to start with this so she went to a bookstore. Besides being comforting bookstores seemed to hold the keys to so much. Mollie was not disappointed. She bought the book <u>A Guide to Farm and Ranch Vacations</u>.

Mollie perused the book which had a description of a multitude of ranches. She picked out five final contenders based on these descriptions and where they were out West. She wrote a short letter to each one and presented her interest in working for them.

The phone rang the next week. It was a ranch in Wyoming. One of their cabin girls had cancelled out and would Mollie be interested in the position? Mollie wanted to shout "Yippee-Ki-Yea!" She accepted the job offer knowing little else.

That night she went over to Judy's place and shared the good news. She tried to sleep on the sofa, but couldn't because tears of joy streamed down her face all night long.

Mollie felt there was one obstacle. She did not think her parents would be as thrilled with this as she was. Mollie made an appointment to see Dr. Minton.

For some reason Dr. Minton gave her blessing to Mollie's adventure. Mollie was relieved. Her parents had the utmost respect for Dr. Minton.

Within two weeks Mollie was off to Wyoming. She was headed for a seventy-five acre ranch in The Snowy Range Pass outside of Laramie. Mollie was looking forward to buying a cowboy hat.

Her plane was greeted by a man who screamed cowboy by looking at him. Tom was bowlegged and he was wearing a checkered shirt. His cowboy hat was black except for its dust. It was shaped haphazardly. Mollie learned that every cowboy's hat was like a signature. Each one was uniquely shaped and one could identify its occupant by looking at them from behind.

At first Mollie thought Tom was chewing gum. After he spit, Mollie realized the gum was chewing tobacco. Otherwise, it would have given a whole new meaning to Juicy Fruit®. One of the caveats of the ranch became, "Don't spit into the sink."

They took the long way around to get to the ranch since the Pass was filled with snow at this time in late May. There were yellow flowers in the miles of meadows they passed.

"What kind of flowers are those?" asked Mollie.

Cowboy Tom was quick. "Those are yellow knee flowers."

Mollie laughed. She felt happy here under the true blue sky with green meadows full of yellow knee flowers. There was no traffic like in Chicago. There were no other vehicles at all. This was the first time Mollie had ever ridden in a pickup truck which happened to be a 4 x 4.

On the ride Mollie learned that Tom and his wife Anne ran the ranch for absentee owners. The couple was originally from Ohio.

Finally they pulled up to the entrance of the Medicine Bow Ranch in the midst of The Medicine Bow National Forest. There was a sign overhanging the entrance which announced the ranch's name to all visitors. A gravel road proceeded from there and wound past four rustic cabins. Rustic meant more primitive than Lincoln Logs.® At the end of the road was the main house and dining room with a kitchen. There was a family area too with a fireplace ready to roar. Beside this main house were two bunk houses. Next to these (much to Mollie's delight) was the corral. A weathered split rail fence contained at least fifteen horses of every size, color, age, and temperament.

Not far from this was a beaver pond with busy beavers engineering dams. A clear stream full of trout ran close by.

Mollie met two of the ranch hands who were about Mollie's age. The guy had been a rodeo rider. The woman had been around horses her entire life and hailed from Cheyenne. They were not overly friendly, but they had no reason to be. This city slicker was on their turf.

The next day Mollie was apprised of her duties. During the day she was to clean the cabins to get them ready for the incoming dudes. The cabins had not been cleaned all fall, winter, or spring. Once the cabins were in shape, Mollie would be in charge of laundering the linens and keeping the cabins clean. In the evening Mollie would waitress the tables. Besides the dudes the town folks would come to eat in the dining room.

Mollie plunged in right away with the cleaning. It seemed like a novelty since she was not used to manual labor. The cabins were filthy. In one bathtub Mollie had to pick up and dispose of dead mice. This was a big deal.

Black dirt covered everything like there was a hole in the floor dispersing dirt. Mollie swept with a broom. This was also something she wasn't accustomed to doing.

Mollie discovered a wonderful machine in the closet. It had round brushes on its underside. When plugged in it whirred and spun. Mollie spun the machine over the dirty floors. It made all the difference. She found out later that it was a floor buffer meant for waxing the floors.

Finally the cabins were ready for the dudes. Before this another ranch hand arrived. He was a sixteen year old kid from St. Louis. His ignorance was revealed one day when he sat atop his horse and said, "Look at this gelding stud!"

Mollie had fun with the waitressing. She was taken to task for asking diners if they wanted ice cubes in their beer.

The cook made her food with love before anyone on TV cooking shows did. She had one specialty that was like Eggs Benedict for breakfast. Many of the women diners balked at the choice.

"That's a lot of calories. I have to watch my weight."

Mollie helped out. "You will burn off the calories three times as fast in this altitude."

Invariably the diner would order it then. Mollie had made up this metabolism story, but it made everyone happy.

At night after the dishes were done Mollie, the cook, and the other cabin girl would pile in a car and head towards Saratoga Springs about a half an hour away. Since they were out in the middle of somewhere, the stars glowed like white Christmas lights. Mollie did not know that stars could look so big.

Once they were in town, they passed the hotel on the corner. This was where Owen Wister stayed to write The Virginian. They drove down the street and past the elevated wooden sidewalks in front of the stores with the fake storefronts. This was the real West.

At the end of the street was their destination. The hot springs were waiting for their tired bodies. The water was an almost tolerable one hundred and eighteen degrees.

Mollie would ease her way into the scalding water. After a few minutes she would hop out. Conveniently next to the springs was the Platte River about six feet away.

Mollie jumped into this fifty-five degree water. It was remarkable that steam did not rise.

Then Mollie went back into the hot springs and any tension was gone after an hour of this process. The drive back to the ranch was always quiet and relaxed as opposed to the boisterous chatter on the way there.

On a few evenings they went to the town's bar. Mollie had her trademark Pepsi® while others might have a beer without ice cubes. The bar's unique feature was a glass display case with stuffed prairie dogs in it. The prairie dogs were in different poses and dressed up like miniature cowboys.

Prairie dogs were plentiful in these parts. They had their own sport. They played chicken with the trucks and cars along the road. It seemed like they waited until a vehicle approached and then the prairie dogs dashed out into the road. It was hard to avoid hitting them no matter how much you swerved. Getting to town without hearing one clunk against a tire was a miracle.

Mollie did witness what seemed like a miracle to her. One afternoon she and the ranch hand were returning from town. The ranch hand spotted a deer in the roadside meadow. The deer began to bound away when the ranch hand and Mollie got out of the truck. The ranch hand gave out some kind of call of the wild. The deer stopped in its hoof steps. The ranch hand said he was half Native American and this was a way of communicating with animals. After a short while the deer moved on.

At that moment a huge bird tried to flap out of a tree in front of them. It mightily tried to lift itself up to fly, but it looked like it was sinking. The bird looked like it weighed fifteen pounds. Suddenly it had an upswing and flowed gracefully into the sky. The ranch hand said it was a golden eagle. It was a golden moment for Mollie. It reminded her of the possibilities in impossibilities.

There was a lot of spare time on the ranch. There was a dearth of dudes. It was the summer of 1979 and the gas shortage was preventing tourists from traveling so much. This gave Mollie more spare time. She went riding as much as she could.

Mollie loved the feel of the leather saddle as much as the scent of the hay around the corral. She was thrilled with how she was trusted to take horses out by herself. After all, it wasn't like checking out books with a library card.

One day she requested to ride a horse named Sleepy. Sleepy was a saddlebred which gave him a one of a kind gait. He also had a tremendous swayback. It was if Santa had sat on him and left a lasting impression.

Mollie was able to prompt Sleepy to cantor for a short distance. When they returned to the ranch entrance, Mollie had to get off Sleepy to open the gate. When she remounted him, the saddle slid and Mollie was practically underneath him. She ended up walking Sleepy back to the barn. The ranch hand said Mollie was lucky not to have been bucked off.

Columbo was Mollie's favorite horse. He was a Paint. His white and chestnut round markings were striking. His body was robust and muscular. He held his head up proudly. He was fast and sure. Columbo epitomized majesty.

The Paint originated with the sixteen war horses that the Spanish Conquistador Hernando Cortes brought to America. Then the Plains tribes began to favor them.

Every Friday the ranch held its own gymkhana. That is a miniature rodeo. The competitions included two kinds of barrel racing and Mollie's favorite musical plates. Dinner plates were put on the corral's ground. Everyone rode around the plates at a slow pace while the ranch hand played his harmonica. If a person's horse were not over a plate when the music stopped, that rider was eliminated. It was musical saddles instead of musical chairs.

Mollie and Colombo did o.k. at this, but did not win. Then the keyhole competition came up. A keyhole shape was limed in at one end of the corral. It was just big enough for a horse to enter, turn around and exit. The horse and rider had to race down to the end of the corral to do this maneuver and then race back to the finish line at the other end of the corral. The horse could not touch the limed marking.

Colombo and Mollie clicked. They charged down the length of the corral and turned quickly around in the keyhole. As they raced back to the finish line, dust kicked up around them. Mollie's hat flew off. Mollie felt invigorated. Columbo deserved an extra carrot stick.

Mollie and Columbo had done the deed in 10.1 seconds. The male ranch hand who had been on the rodeo circuit competed next. He ran his graphite colored steed full force down the corral. He pulled back on the reins in the keyhole to give his horse a clean turn. They took a full gallop back to the finish line. His time was announced. The cowboy had beaten Mollie and Columbo by one tenth of a second. In victory he spat out some tobacco juice.

During the last week of June it snowed. All the ranch activities were suspended. The ranch managers put on Christmas music and some heat. A fire was set in the fireplace and hot chocolate was passed out.

Normally it was seventy degrees and sunny during the day. The evenings were pleasant too. One evening

Mollie and some of the other workers decided to go to a street dance several towns over from the ranch. This was a dance with a band that was held in the town's street. When Mollie arrived, there were only a few people wandering in the street. There was no band. Mollie wondered what had happened.

True to the lore of the Old West someone had been shot earlier while in the street. Mollie could see men with wide push brooms sweeping up.

This was such a different world than back in Chicago. The male ranch hand related a story about horse trading. He said that if a horse were malnourished, a trader would give it a little bit of arsenic which plumped out the horse until it was sold.

On the Fourth of July a number of the ranch people rode in the 4 x 4 pickup to the top of Kennaday Peak. They drove over brush and streaming river beds. At the top of the mountain they intended to have a good view of the fireworks. They waited hours and there were no explosives. It was discovered later that the man in charge of the fireworks took the money for them and used it for something else.

Mollie had been to the top of the peak once before this. Snow was all around. Mollie and the others had taken cardboard and sledded down the sides of the mountain. The fun lasted as long as the cardboard.

Business became worse at the ranch. Mollie was asked to leave. The kid from St. Louis was also bid Adios.

Mollie had the time of her life. She was thankful for the experience. After returning to Chicago Mollie continued to wear her cowboy hat out of habit and pride.

She was able to get her mental health technician job back. Judy and she had grown more distant. Judy had made a couple of new friends plus she was engaged. Mollie and Judy's backgammon games never resumed like they had before this.

Mollie continued to work for Dr. Wontherr. One fall day his social worker approached Mollie and asked her if she would like to join her and the doctor to go hot air ballooning. This did not call for hesitation. Mollie accepted the invitation. It did not make any difference in her decision when she found out that she had to be at the balloon launch site at 5 A.M.

When Mollie arrived at the balloon launching site, the flattened balloons were on the ground. Fans were blowing air into the limp material. It was like CPR for these balloons as they inflated and came to life. Their bright colors cheered on the passengers. The designs on the balloons were geometric and in primary colors. It was like looking at what would be floating crayons.

A rugged straw basket was attached to the balloon. It was quite a stretch for Mollie to lift her leg over the side to tumble inside. The psychiatrist and the social worker did the same.

A flame was turned on and off above their heads to keep the air hot and to power the balloon. They slowly lifted up and silently drifted through the morning sky. It was daybreak and even though most of the world was awakening, the balloon occupants were wide awake with wonder.

In the air the balloon hung down like an oblong gum ball. Its colors clashed with the sunrise.

Soon the balloon scooted into farm country. They were soaring above a turkey farm with the gobbling clearly audible. The bark of a dog sounded.

Dr. Wontherr pulled out some chocolate from his pocket and passed it around. He said that when he was a boy in Germany, balloonists would land in the fields nearby. He and the other children would run out to greet them. The balloonists always had chocolate to give to the excited children.

The balloon was high at this point and going at the rapid clip of fifteen miles per hour. Dr. Wontherr peered over the side of the basket and said, "MY GOD, I think I'm hallucinating!"

The balloon pilot quickly commanded, "Get down!" Everybody huddled on the floor of the basket. They had just missed a high tension wire.

Then they landed in a marsh. A sheriff's car arrived on the scene. "Someone reported a balloon crashing." The sheriff was probably relieved that he did not have to file an accident report or have any injuries on his hands.

This experience and the dude ranch were two of the highlights of Mollie's life. She was happy and it wasn't due to any energy being fueled by a mental illness.

Mollie never knew what a new day would bring. Every day at work was an improvisation.

During an afternoon shift the charge nurse asked Mollie to go to the ice cream shop and bring back ice cream. The other staff member told Mollie what kind of milkshake she wanted and off went Mollie.

It took forever at the ice cream shop. It was summer and the shop was packed with people. The one shake machine wobbled as it churned. It was as inefficient as the service. Mollie must have waited forty-five minutes. It was worth the wait because ice cream is a psychological necessity.

Mollie lugged the frozen prizes back to the hospital. She walked onto the psychiatric unit and the other two staff members were not around. Mollie did not blame them for giving up on the ice cream, but typically the nurse was at the nursing station. Mollie waited, but all that was happening was that the ice cream was melting.

Then she heard it. A noise was coming from down the hallway. Mollie walked towards it. The sound was coming from a door. There was pounding and yelling. Mollie realized this was the Quiet Room where patients were put in seclusion and put in restraints if needed. A peephole in the door reveals what is going on inside.

Mollie took a look. A patient was on the bed in restraints. The nurse and the other staff member were making the noise inside.

Taking out her keys Mollie unlocked the door. She entered the room and said, "What are you guys doing in here?"

Before anyone could react, the big door swung shut. Now all of them were locked inside the room. Liquified ice cream was the least of their troubles.

The three staff members pounded on the door and yelled. Finally the music therapist was walking by and heard their distress. That's when perfect pitch comes in handy. He freed the grateful three. Mollie was probably the only one who had been locked up before.

Mollie was seeing Dr. Minton once a month or less. During one session Dr. Minton confronted Mollie.

"Do you want to be a mental health tech for the rest of your life?"

Mollie had not given it much thought. They talked about Mollie's options. Obtaining a Masters in Social Work seemed like a workable idea.

The Jane Addams School of Social Work in downtown Chicago at The University of Illinois attracted Mollie. It had a stellar reputation and Mollie could afford it if she applied for a student loan. The catch was that Mollie had one week to get all of her application material submitted before the next session began.

Mollie filled out the long application and Dr. Wontherr agreed to provide one of the recommendations. Mollie somehow met the deadline. Except for becoming a cheerleader Mollie always came through in a crunch.

During the first week of school John Kendricks died. His mother had died in the prior year. John had died of cirrhosis of the liver. Happy hours had done him in.

Mollie had limited experience with death. Her grandparents Elmer and Emma Skilss had died years earlier. Mollie attended both of their funerals. Grandma Emma died of a brutal death from gastric cancer. She withered away when the country doctor's treatment of having her drink vodka failed. She was in her early sixties when death took her away.

Grandpa Elmer died in his sleep when he was seventy-four years old. No one had seen him for a few days. Someone forced their way into the farmhouse and found him in bed. Mollie knew that many say this is "the way to go." Mollie did not think most ways were "the best way to go." Death awed her.

She remembered Grandpa Elmer urging her to put on her coat one snowy, winter day. Mollie pulled on her shiny red boots and trudged out to the barn with Grandpa Elmer. He was carrying a rifle. Mollie was twelve years old and this was the first time that Grandpa Elmer had ever asked her to do anything with him.

They were at the Dutch door that looked into the stable of cows. The top half of the door was open. Mollie could barely see over it, but she could see enough. Grandpa Elmer aimed the gun above the cows and fired. Splat went a rat. It fell to its death. Without a word Grandpa Elmer and Mollie trekked back to the farmhouse. She did not mention the incident to anyone, but thought it was strange.

Guilt grabbed her with John's death. She would miss too much school if she went to his memorial service. Mollie decided not to go. She had many happy memories of John and that would be her way of memorializing him.

Sanwadoon's era was over.

CHAPTER 14

Earning her M.S.W. (Masters in Social Work) was time consuming. In her bedroom Mollie had books piled up and papers scattered everywhere. She was a conscientious student and managed to get A's and B's. Somehow she managed to work at Woods Hospital part-time too.

Doing this work at Woods Hospital and her background in group therapy served her well in her studies. Mollie managed to place out of a couple of classes.

The M.S.W. program was small. There were close to one hundred students. This was the type of small pond that Mollie liked being a fish in. She was able to entertain her classmates with her humor.

In her Psychopathology class she had to give a case presentation. Mollie was not well prepared and decided to improvise it. She was tense which partly explained what happened.

Mollie told about a counseling client she had who was from some Eastern European country. The woman had a heavy accent. Her problem was her elderly mother who "would not go oot."

Mollie said she tried to clarify the problem. "She won't go out?"

"She won't go oot."

Mollie tried again. "She won't go out anywhere? She won't go out to the grocery store?"

"No, she won't go OOT."

Now Mollie started to laugh. She was so nervous. Her laughter was contagious. The whole class was laughing.

Mollie said she figured out what "going oot" meant. The elderly woman was constipated. The class erupted.

The professor loved it. He used it as an object lesson to illustrate the point that the crazier that the underlying theme is then the funnier it is on the surface for inexplicable reasons.

On the first day of class in another course the professor was taking roll call. He would call a name and the student would say, "Present, but I like to be called Maggie."

The professor explained he was taking attendance and did not need nicknames. He called another name. "Present, but I like to be called Bob."

The professor lost his cool demeanor and became cold. "I don't care what you want to be called. I'm taking attendance."

He called a name. "Present, but I like to be called Sandy..."

The professor clenched his teeth. He called Mollie's name. "Present, but I like to be called Bozo."

The impasse was broken. The professor could now "go oot."

After one class a professor asked Mollie to stay. He sat on top of a desk directly in front of Mollie. It was a short and memorable meeting. The professor gave her a one sentence piece of advice and the meeting was over. He said to her, "Never let anyone take away who you are."

It was another thing for Mollie to wonder about.

The M.S.W. studies were a two year program. Because a thesis was not required, two internships were expected to complete the degree. Mollie's speciality was Mental Health Treatment so she did her second internship at the Veterans Administration of North Chicago.

It was about an hour commute one way. Mollie was motivated.

The first time that Mollie drove into the V.A. grounds, she was half frightened. Scattered across the lawn were bodies of men. She later found out that these were veterans who were stretched out on the grass and taking naps.

Since it was summer, some homeless vets migrated from the south to come north. In the winter they did the opposite where they went south to the warmer climate. There were other adjustments Mollie had to make in her thinking while she interned there.

There was a ward where Mollie only went to once. She had to be accompanied by two burly men. There was a puddle of urine on the floor. One man was rocking back and forth. A screened in porch was attached to the main dayroom. It had bars over it and men were clinging and climbing the bars while they screamed and moaned. It was like a scene from the movie "The Snake Pit" only this was real.

On a higher functioning ward Mollie was assigned to follow up with a large man. He was in his early fifties and walked with a cane. He had some sort of issues with his mother, but Mollie was not Freudian enough to know their depth. She would pace the hallway with him because she believed it helped build rapport between them.

Mollie learned this at Woods Hospital. At times the patients would order pizza. As a nurse taught Mollie, "Always take a piece of pizza if they offer it to you. It builds rapport."

Every day Mollie would walk the hallway with this hefty man. One day she asked an innocuous question, but it must not have been. The man lifted his cane over his head in the striking position.

Mollie cringed, cowered and yelled, "Don't hit me!"

Maybe because they had some rapport built, the man slowly lowered the cane to his side. That was the end of their walks.

The V.A. was where Mollie learned about nosocomial disease. One could get it by touching a doorknob. The disease referred to fecal or other bacteria being present on surfaces and infecting those who touched those surfaces.

Mollie was grossed out about this possibility. She lived on ice cream from a vending machine for her lunches instead of going to the cafeteria. Because she did not have time in the morning before her commute, she did not pack a lunch.

There was another patient whom Mollie followed. He was a short, black man with a weathered face. He had an intensity when he looked at Mollie. Missing teeth offset the gleaming white ones that he had left. The man readily engaged on a verbal basis with Mollie. Suddenly in the middle of their conversation the man stopped what he was saying. He looked sharply at Mollie and proclaimed, "You are from another planet!" That was the end of their interview.

Mollie told her supervisor about this odd remark. The supervisor was quick to point out that Mollie should have asked him, "Which planet?"

The bizarreness did not end here. Mollie joined the V.A. softball team. It was coed and competitive like coed competition is.

At first Mollie caused consternation with the opposing team when she hit the ball and slid into first base. She was called out mainly because it was an unorthodox way to play. Mollie suspected it had something to do with being a girl.

Mollie played first base. A man who was the size of a dump truck came running down the line and ran over Mollie. Mollie hit the dirt face down. The next thing she was aware of were feet and legs encircling her. She groaned. A woman helped pick her up and grabbed her by the arm. Mollie limped around the ball field in her grasp. She told this woman teammate that she was o.k. The woman said, "Not yet. Make the other team think about what they did to you. Play it for all its worth."

She was not a drama queen, but Mollie followed the woman's advice. On the side lines the dump truck guy was being chastised for running over a girl. He was instructed to give Mollie an apology.

Another diversion was the time when Mollie and her supervisor took patients in the day program to the Wisconsin State Fair. On the morning bus ride there the supervisor talked about how she was looking forward to eating a bratwurst and funnel cake. The supervisor stopped short of salivating.

They arrived at the fair in its full glory of sounds, colors, and smells. Flashing lights alerted fair goers to the rides. Pungent onions mixed with the odors of sweet baked goods caused an addictive craving.

Mollie's supervisor ran over to the bratwurst booth and gobbled down the sandwich. Then she found a funnel cake and washed it down with a diet cola. That was breakfast.

Mollie and her supervisor wandered the grounds. The midway was not crowded at this time of day. Then the supervisor spotted it.

"Let's go on that ride!" It was a ride with an arm perpendicular to the ground with a cage attached to the end of the arm. Mollie and her supervisor climbed into the caged enclosure where they had to stand next to each other. The ride operator fired up the ride which lifted them into the air. They had a momentary bird's eye view of the fair grounds before the cage went topsy turvy and the ride's arm rotated them around. The speed picked up. Then the unthinkable flew forth. The supervisor's breakfast spewed out. It was a vomit comet that would not stop.

Mollie could not be empathetic even though she had suffered with motion sickness all of her life. She yelled at her supervisor, "Turn the other way!"

To get the operator to stop the ride Mollie kept yelling, STOP!" The operator must have thought these were shouts of glee since it was another two minutes until he shut the ride down.

Not only was the supervisor feeling ill, but she was embarrassed. Mollie never brought it up again. Neither did the supervisor---literally or figuratively.

To get through school Mollie applied for a job at Lord & Taylor. She was told there were no positions open. Mollie went back a second time and a third time to see if this had changed. It hadn't. On her fourth try the personnel lady hired her because of Mollie's persistence.

She was put to work in the store's jewelry department. One of the instructions she was given was to only wait on one customer at a time. This became time consuming when the customer was window shopping. People patiently waited so Mollie knew that she could too.

The security folks in plain clothes hung around to protect the valuable merchandise. They carefully watched everything.

One weekend Mollie requested to have off. That Sunday morning the employees came in and all the jewelry cases had been emptied. Everyone except Mollie had to undergo a polygraph exam. The culprits were caught. The security folks had committed the crime.

Mollie never knew what was going to happen there next. She was transferred to work in the glove and hosiery department. For one transaction a man handed over his credit card. He was accompanying his blonde wife. It was a department where men did not frequent. This guy was not only distinguished looking, but a good sport. Mollie looked down at the credit card. It read "Conrad Hilton."

He was the most famous person that Mollie had encountered up until now. Her father was more likely to run into famous people.

Bud was playing a golf course in Wisconsin with colleagues. He hit a shot way off into the rough. He was lining up his shot in the midst of nowhere when he heard a golf cart coming in his direction. Bud looked up to see a guy wave and say, "Hi, Bud."

It was Jack Nicklaus.

Bud's colleagues swore that they had nothing to do with the incident. They finally admitted that Nicklaus had happened by them and agreed when asked to participate in the joke. Bud was happy with Nicklaus's greeting, but wished he had not been in the rough at the time.

Mollie had her bout with fame as she approached the completion of her degree. She applied and was accepted to be included in the book A Gentleman's Guide to Single Women in Chicago.

She was not deluged with mail as she had hoped. After all, there were ninety-nine other women to choose from in the book. It was a buffet for men.

One man whom she heard from lived a half hour away in Chicago. He did not have a car and wanted Mollie to pick him up for their date. That letter went into the round file. He wrote again with a desperate edge to his letter. It gave Mollie the creeps. She disposed of this letter faster than the first.

Mollie wrote to a man in <u>A Woman's Guide to Single Men in Chicago</u>. He was overweight in a teddy bear sort of way. Jerry contacted her without wasting time. He was a Mormon with a sense of humor and a sense of playfulness. Their first date was on Valentine's Day. Jerry brought Mollie fudge that he had made. Mollie gave him chocolates that were foil wrapped to look like sardines. They were off to an auspicious start.

Even though he lived a short distance away in Chicago, Jerry wrote letters to Mollie. They had a fun correspondence. Jerry was imaginative.

His friends were creative also. He invited Mollie to their Academy Award night. Some of the people had made comedy videos to show. The audience voted on the winner.

The one Mollie liked was about a guy who was going through a cafeteria line. The guy passed by the green gelatin. The gelatin leaped off its plate and onto the guy's chest. He ended up screaming on the floor. The killer gelatin was the last camera shot. It was seen jiggling on the guy's chest.

Jerry met Mollie's parents. He told Bud how he had gone to The Playboy Mansion once. Jerry described the scene more than Mollie would have liked, but it was a G-rated version.

Mollie did not talk about what happened during her freshman year of high school. In one of her classes a girl had a clutch of students around her. The girl was crying.

"What's going on?" Mollie asked the student next to her.

"Christie is telling people that Hugh Hefner is her father."

It was true. Her parents were divorced and Christie lived with her mother, brother, and stepfather.

Jerry and Mollie looked alike. They both had black hair and blue eyes. Except for the Mormon business they were a match.

One thing that freaked Jerry out were the suburbs. Where Mollie lived, he called it the country. "What do you do if you get a flat tire?" Jerry said it felt eerie to him like the movie "Halloween." He was a city guy and his imagination was not a help in the suburbs.

Jerry was on the rebound when he met Mollie. Eventually he bounced back to his former fiancee and they married. Almost thirty years later Mollie learned that he was making a living by selling auction items online.

Mollie's infatuation with Jerry was the type where she would be driving and completely get lost. She was preoccupied with him. Missing him was a slow bleed.

Around this time was when Mollie began to hole up in her bedroom. She had moved back into her parent's house after returning from the ranch. While Mollie was in her room, she started to write one-liners. She typed pages of her brand of comedy.

One day Helen looked in on Mollie. "Why don't you send your material to someone?"

Mollie found out that Phyllis Diller was going to be in Chicago performing. Mollie sent two pages of jokes to the club where Diller was going to appear.

Months later Mollie received a check for the sale of two jokes from Phyllis Diller. Diller had made a notation in pencil: "Puns are the lowest form of humor."

Mollie wanted to write back to say, "Jokes about feet are the lowest form of humor." She didn't because it illustrated Phyllis Diller's point.

Armed and elbowed with this success Mollie wrote to Joan Rivers when she was scheduled to be in Chicago. Mollie was ecstatic when she received a check from her for a comedy sale.

Not too long after this Mollie went to see Joan Rivers perform in a local night club. After Joan performed, she had what looked like a receiving line off to the side of the stage. Mollie joined the line. When she greeted Joan, she did not want to let the moment slip away.

"I sold you a joke."

"Tell it to me."

Mollie faltered as she delivered the joke. It was not one of her one-liners. It was considerably longer.

Joan interrupted to fill in the punchline. Mollie smiled weakly. Joan was nothing like her stage presence. She complimented Mollie. "You must be very talented. I never buy material the first time they send it in."

Mollie looked at this flawless face. Her complexion looked like a porcelain doll. She appeared to be a minus size two. Mollie was grateful to this lady who could have ripped her to shreds. She said her thanks and moved on like in a daydream.

After this, Mollie decided to polish her comedy skills. She took two improvisation classes associated with

Second City in Chicago. She also performed at open microphone nights at comedy clubs. Being afraid of forgetting her lines terrified her more than being in front of a large audience. She started out by getting polite silence and eventually getting the club to burst out in loud laughter. It depended what kind of crowd was there. Mollie knew she did not have the motorcycle gang crowd in the palm of her hand. Maybe it was because she worked clean. Maybe it was because they didn't understand her jokes. Maybe it was because she wasn't that good. Mollie wasn't sure.

Mollie wondered about something else. She was in the audience of a comedy club one night and a British man unexpectedly stood up and started yelling. He was not an act.

"We won the War by using your money and our brains!" The bouncers were on top of him faster than clotted cream.

Much as Mollie enjoyed comedy, she went the traditional route after earning her M.S.W. It didn't take her long to be hired at an adolescent and family treatment agency. She arranged to begin after she took a trip out West.

Mollie booked a trip on the Amtrak train that chugged its way to Glacier National Park in Montana. Then Mollie made reservations to stay in a lodge there on the shores of a lake.

The train trip whizzed by except for the food. At that time the food was dripping with grease and was composed of cholesterol. Mollie was not one for eating healthy foods, yet she found herself craving fresh fruits and vegetables.

Mollie did not have a sleeper car. She sat up in her seat to snooze. Comfort was not a choice at this point.

Arriving at Glacier National Park was the highlight of the trip. It was September and the snowy peaks did not need a Chamber of Commerce to greet visitors. The air tasted fresh. Pine trees dotted the mountain slopes. Shades of green on the lower elevations outdid Ohio's hues. Mollie thought to herself that this is America's Switzerland.

The lodge was made out of huge light brown beams. Native American blankets were hanging down from the inside second story balcony. A herd of elk and deer heads were mounted on the walls. Comfortable overstuffed chairs filled the lobby. On the outside porch were wooden rocking chairs. Mollie went to her room and slept like a hibernating bear.

The next morning Mollie went to the dining room and had a greaseless breakfast. She went outside and shot photos of the lake. She came inside and took photos of the lodge's interior.

The rental horses had left the day before because the season was over. This was a major disappointment to Mollie. This meant she would be forced to go hiking.

The thought of hiking by herself was daunting. She was afraid of being confronted by a bear. Mollie did not handle any confrontation well much less with a bear. Mollie recalled a park ranger's piece of wisdom about bears. "Even if you can't see them; they can see you."

Mollie started out by herself. Making noise to warn the bears she was around also made her feel safer. Mollie sang and whistled.

She heard something. She stopped.

It was humans. More specifically it was a couple who were Mollie's age. They suggested hiking together. Mollie had no objection.

They encountered no bears or other wildlife. Everyone agreed to have dinner at the lodge. Until Mollie left, they spent a good amount of time together. They were Mollie's guardian angels.

The day came for Mollie to leave on Amtrak. She stood on the wooden train platform in the middle of the park's forest. It was the last day Glacier was going to be open for the season. Mollie waited beyond the arrival time of the train. Something was wrong.

Word arrived that Amtrak had gone on strike. This was one of the last trains running in the country. Amtrak executives were engineering it.

The train finally pulled up with its loud brakes underscoring how things had stopped. Mollie stepped onto the train. She and the other passengers were told that any stop could be their last. They would be bused home from there if that should happen. As they drew closer to Minneapolis, they were told that this was the last Amtrak train running in the entire United States. T.V. camera crews met the train in Minneapolis.

Mollie wanted to get home in time to start her new job. It isn't good form to miss the first day of work. The greasy food and her adrenalin were not the best mix.

They pulled into Chicago. The train was late. Mollie didn't care. She was going to make it to work on time.

The next day Mollie showed up for her new job. She was going to do family counseling and counseling with adolescents. It was a small staff of four other counselors. The supervisor tended to have an unreasonable side. One time she took Mollie to task for never saying, "Good morning." Mollie wondered about this since no one there ever gave this greeting.

Mollie tried to fit in by drinking coffee for the first time in her life. She poured a half cup of powdered creamer in a styrofoam cup along with several packets of sugar. Covering this with coffee made it almost palatable for Mollie. She was unsure why she wasn't reprimanded for this indulgence. Mollie quickly learned that coffee was not her friend. It triggered violent diarrhea.

Mollie fit in at this agency as well as she fit in the fifth grade. The therapist she shared an office with was friendly on a professional basis. He taught Mollie how to fill out government forms. Ted instructed her.

"Make sure you check every box and fill out every line. Don't leave anything blank."

At lunch Mollie walked around the neighborhood. She discovered a bonanza of a yard sale during one of these walks. For a quarter she bought a taxidermist's stuffed dolphin fish. Mollie hung it over the sofa in her office to remind herself not to take things too seriously when she was doing family therapy. It worked. It caused another worry. Mollie was afraid it might fall during a session and clunk a family member on the head. That was the end of that fishing expedition. Mollie took the fish home.

Mollie had live fish before this. A patient at Woods Hospital gave her a pair of Black Mollies. To keep them safe until she went home Mollie took the plastic bag of water they were in and hung them from an IV stand.

The summer Olympics were in full swing. Her fish were nameless, but had a good home in a fish bowl. Mollie left them to adjust to their new abode while she watched the gymnastics competition on TV. Olga Korbut was phenomenal. After the medals were awarded, Mollie went upstairs to her room. One of the fish was missing.

Mollie looked closely. There was a black mass stuck to the wall. The fish had leaped out of the bowl. Mollie peeled the fish off the wall and plopped it back into the bowl's water. Now the fish had a name: Olga. Olga went on to have a long life in fish years and mothered thirty-four offspring.

Mollie felt like a fish out of water herself at the agency where she didn't think she was doing a terrific job at counseling. Over a year after she began there, Mollie resigned.

It did not take long for Mollie to find another job. She was hired as a telemarketer for law books at a legal publishing company. The rejection wasn't hard to take since she was used to it. Mollie made enough sales to keep her job. Then she took a proofreading test and was promoted to preparing legal manuscripts for publication.

It was quiet work which exercised her brain. She liked it even with the low pay. Socially she made many friends and acquaintances. A bunch of them went to see her perform at a comedy club. Having this amount of acceptance was something Mollie had lacked for a while.

Around this time Helen found an ad in the local weekly newspaper The Winnetka Talk. The ad wanted volunteers for a study. A parent and an offspring with a diagnosis of schizophrenia were needed. Helen and Mollie agreed it would be a good idea.

The study was being done at The V.A. of North Chicago where Mollie had done her M.S.W. internship. She felt her cheeks get warm as she hoped she wouldn't see anyone she knew there.

Norman Rosenthal, M.D. greeted them. He went on to do landmark studies on Seasonal Affective Disorder at The National Institute for Mental Health.

Helen and Mollie were separated for the tests. Mollie was given a MRI of her brain. Then she was shown rapid slides and asked to react to them with a push button.

The results came in. Dr. Rosenthal gave Mollie his verdict.

"There's no way you are schizophrenic. If anything, you are manic depressive."

Mollie's suspicions were confirmed. That was why she had racing thoughts, feelings of tremendous energy, mood swings, and irritability. Her paranoid delusions were from lack of sleep instead of from some type of schizophrenic process. Mollie was looking forward to discussing this with Dr. Minton.

At thirty years old Mollie had reached two milestones. One was being diagnosed correctly and the other was getting her ears pierced for the first time.

Dr. Minton agreed to treat Mollie with the drug of choice at that time for manic depression. It was Lithium™. Lithium is a salt that is naturally found in the human body. For a while it was one of the ingredients of the soft drink 7-Up®. It wasn't until 1969 that Lithium™ was an approved medication in the United States.

In a study a group of British psychiatrists and a group of American psychiatrists were shown films of patients. For the same patients the British psychiatrists diagnosed them as manic depressive whereas the American psychiatrists diagnosed them as schizophrenic. It was a tricky diagnosis to distinguish.

Mollie started taking Lithium™ with no other medication. Helen noticed a difference immediately.

"I have my old Mollie back."

Bud approached Mollie one day. "I want you to have this." He handed her the black walnut and added, "I got this at the LBJ ranch."

"I didn't know you were ever there."

Bud offered no more explanation. Mollie took the walnut and preserved it by putting it into a small plastic sandwich bag.

At work one of her buddies lent her a book. Mollie's pet peeve was when people did not return books that they had borrowed from her.

This buddy talked about how he was able to get into the club "21" when he was in New York. He said he had a friend there. Mollie wondered how he managed to get into that club because he was short, squat, and nondescript.

She called up her buddy to return the borrowed book. He lived with his parents. Mollie knew his father was a Chicago judge. The buddy told her to come on over.

It took Mollie five minutes to drive over to his house. The doorbell chimed its rich, deep tones. Her buddy did not answer the door. Instead, a dark, tall, and handsome young man opened the door. He smiled cordially and took the book. Mollie did not realize until she left who it was. This was not a delusion. This was John F. Kennedy Jr.

CHAPTER 15

Mollie missed her counseling work. She interviewed at an elegant retirement home just down the block from Dr. Minton's home. As Mollie entered the place The Fountain, she noticed an old man dressed in a jacket and a tie. He looked like he was waiting for nothing in particular and had a strained look on his face. He did not return the smile that Mollie gave him.

Upon entering the lobby Mollie was impressed with the trappings. A fountain predominated over the room. The splash of water energized the sedate quietness. Oriental rugs lined the floor. Corinthian columns arose from the carpets to the high ceilings. Mollie was entranced.

There were a few elderly women wheeling around the area with their walkers and canes. So far Mollie liked what she saw.

The Director came out and introduced himself to Mollie. His interview was interesting. It did not have much depth, but Mollie's resume lacked depth. He told her that the building had once been a hotel owned by a famous Chicago hotelier and this had been the tycoon's favorite hotel. When the hotelier sold the hotel to the retirement place, the agreement was that the labor union would stay intact there. The labor union's membership consisted of the nurse's aides, the housekeepers, and the kitchen staff.

Mollie was given a tour and she was taken by the dining room. There was a huge crystal chandelier that lit the room along with the wall sconces. White tablecloths covered all of the tables. The walls were painted Mollie's favorite shade of light sky blue with French windows trimmed in white. The lunch that was cooking made Mollie's tummy react with longing.

Mollie would have her work cut out for her. The retirement home was nine stories high with an Assisted Living wing and an entire floor that was for Advanced Health Care.

Driving home Mollie felt good about her chances. A social work professor told her once, "You will never have trouble finding a job." What Mollie wasn't told was that she would have trouble keeping a job...

The call came. Mollie accepted the position as Director of Social Work.

On her first day at The Fountain Mollie noticed the Director carrying a cardboard box out the door. One of the staff made an oblique comment. Mollie expressed some curiosity.

"This is his last day." Mollie was spared the details.

These weren't the only details that Mollie was spared. The day before Mollie started her employment, the older man she had noted in the foyer had jumped to his death from the ninth floor. The staff looked like they were in shock. Apparently the man was depressed over having macular degeneration of his eyes. He had to give up activities he loved such as golf. He left a widow who was not willing to speak with Mollie.

Mollie's main job was to interview potential residents for The Fountain. Besides the writing of life stories Mollie enjoyed the interaction with the older folks. She found the advice intriguing too.

"Travel while you're young" was one piece of wisdom that was imparted. Another caution she was given had to do with staving off depression. More than one woman told her, "Keep busy."

One old woman caught her off guard. The woman asked Mollie, "Do you know why people don't like old people?"

"No, why not?"

The woman took the flab under her upper arm and swung it back and forth.

Mollie laughed. The Lithium™ did not stop her from having a sense of humor.

There was another woman whom Mollie visited in her resident apartment. The woman had a grand piano in the middle of her living room. Her living room had a picturesque view of Lake Michigan. The woman had newspapers piled up throughout the living room. Mollie asked the woman if she played her piano anymore. The answer was no. Mollie thought it would be a good idea for her to play again.

From home Mollie brought an elementary duet piano book. She sat down at the grand piano next to the woman who had not played for a long time. Mollie had not played in a while either. They began to plunk the keys. Mollie played wrong notes and was quite bad. The two of them played on and laughed.

Subsequently the woman was diagnosed as having dementia and died soon after that. Reading her obituary Mollie was shocked to find out that the woman had performed at Carnegie Hall by playing the piano.

Mollie was shocked and appalled by other matters at The Fountain. The racial divide interfered with care. All of the unionized workers were black and the heads of all of the departments were white.

A resident in the Advanced Health Care area confided in Mollie that the nursing aides were blackmailing the residents. If the resident refused to pay the aide a certain amount of money, then the resident would not get their basic needs met.

Mollie called the work at The Fountain as "working with the healthy and the wealthy." There was a lot of money to be had in blackmailing.

Mollie approached the new Director. He feared the union. His tires had "mysteriously" been flattened more than once. His decision was to do nothing.

Crowd pressure also existed at the resident level. A woman came in to see Mollie. She was a new resident and had planted a tomato plant in the garden on the premises. A couple of other women who lived there gave this woman a hard time about it and said that only flowers were allowed to be planted there. Mollie encouraged the woman to stand firm and by the middle of the summer Mollie had a nice sized tomato for her support.

The staff had their own set of problems. The head of maintenance came to chat with Mollie.

He started with an attention getter. "I saw Jesus today."

"Where did you see him?"

"By my car where I park here. Jesus gave me messages to give to people who work here."

"What are they?"

"I can't tell you. They are for staff."

"Did Jesus give you a message for me?"

"No."

That was the end of their discussion. Mollie was disappointed that Jesus did not have greetings for her.

Mollie was enamored with one of the activities workers. Bob had a terrific sense of humor and was a Christian. Mollie participated in a Bible Study with him after work. She had a crush on him which was only returned with unserious flirting.

One morning Mollie was running late to work. She swooped into a parking spot in front of The Fountain. As she hurriedly exited her car, Bob was there and quipped, "And here is Mollio Andretti."

Mollie gave speeches to inform and entertain the residents. After her second speech Bob approached her and said, "You lead people right to the edge of the cliff and then stop in the nick of time."

Mollie smiled. She took this as a compliment.

Bob was talented musically and had the starring role of Jesus in a local production of Godspell. Along with several residents Mollie attended the musical. She transported residents back to The Fountain. Her car was small and one elderly woman had a time of it in getting out of the car. Her other problems were not as obvious. Once she was extricated from the car, Mollie noticed a brown spot where the woman had been seated.

Mollie had fun at her job. One day she put her telephone in her top desk drawer. Her lamp was placed on top of the desk above this drawer. She put the department head of housekeeping on the speaker phone. Voila! She had a talking lamp.

Mollie called the Assistant Director in and began asking the lamp questions. The lamp dutifully answered. The Assistant Director was so excited that she ran into the hall. She called to a resident who was there.

"Mrs. Brewer, come see the talking lamp."

Mrs. Brewer hobbled into Mollie's office. The Assistant Director began asking the lamp questions. There was no response. It was terribly funny at the time.

Mollie was put in charge of a team meeting of some of the department heads including the dietician. For some perverse reason Mollie inflated a Whoopee Cushion® and placed it under a real sofa cushion in her office. Everyone came to the meeting and randomly sat down. No one sat where the Whoopee Cushion® was hidden. The dietician was the last to arrive.

"I'm sorry I'm late," she said. "I had to deal with a delivery of cabbage."

With perfect timing she sat down and the Whoopee Cushion® did its job. Mollie was as pleased as much as the dietician was chagrined.

Meanwhile, Mollie became more involved at church. First, she had a class of three year olds and was instructed to just make it fun so that they would want to come to Sunday School.

One Sunday Mollie did what she thought would create a cheerful ambiance. Since a preschool met in her Sunday School classroom during the week, there was secular music around. Mollie put on the "Beer Barrel Polka" which is not exactly Methodist music. Much to Mollie's horror, church was let out early and the parents dropped in to pick up their kids as the polka played in full force.

Then Mollie taught a class of four and five year olds. She taught them the song "We are Fishers of Men." After running through the verses a couple of times, one little boy flipped up his necktie and declared, "Look, I caught a trout."

To demonstrate the celebration of Christmas in Mexico Mollie had a pinata loaded with candy for the kids. She blindfolded them and gave them a small broom to try and smash open the pinata. No one was having any success.

Parents started filtering in to pick up their children. A parent took the broom and wanted to be blindfolded. He flailed away. Another father finally connected. He beat the bejabbers out of the pinata. Mollie thought how much violence there was in a place meant to promote peace.

Mollie continued to take Adult Enrichment classes at night. In one class a guy she really didn't know approached her and asked, "How does it feel to have your father be President?" Mollie did not respond. She did not know what to say. The guy walked away.

At work Mollie was running into difficulty. The Director was acting strange. The Accountant said the Director was being irresponsible with the facility's money. In a staff meeting the Director made the remark, "I would show you what self-love is, but I don't have enough room." It was clearly a sexual remark.

Mollie talked about his condition with the consulting psychiatrist whom Mollie had lobbied successfully to be hired by The Fountain. She wasn't sure in talking with him that anything would be done.

Apparently the psychiatrist did talk with the Director. Mollie became the Director's target. Within two months she was fired with no cause.

Mollie spent months and months sending out resumes and going on interviews. She was going nowhere fast even though she drove to Port Huron, Michigan and back for a job interview.

She finally found an ad in the national social work newspaper for a position in Florida. She flew to Tampa Bay and interviewed at a small, psychiatric hospital. The job was offered to her before she left and she accepted.

Mollie arrived home and the telephone was ringing as soon as she stepped inside the door. When she answered it, she had another job offer to be on a crisis team. Mollie turned it down. The next day she had another job offer which she also refused. In three weeks she would be driving to move to Tampa Bay.

Mollie was thirty-six years old. Except for college and almost a year in her Chicago apartment Mollie had never lived away from home for any length of time. Her sister-in-law expressed disbelief that Mollie would move so far away.

Mollie felt like she had to because of the job situation and to be less enmeshed with her family. On the day she left she stuffed her tiny car that had the brown spot on the back seat. She had her teddy bear on the front seat beside her. Helen had bought it for her when Mollie had lost her job. When Helen brought it home, Mollie thought it was for one of her nieces or nephews. She was delighted to find it was for her.

She arrived in Tampa Bay on the eve of her thirty-seventh birthday. The drive across the brilliantly blue and sparkling Tampa Bay was a treat. It was a sunny March day. It was a lucky day too as Mollie found an oldies 60's station on her car radio. She checked into a motel that had seen better days and nights.

On the following night the motel operator cut off Mollie's incoming phone calls after nine o'clock. The motel operator did not care that it was Mollie's birthday or else it was her version of an April Fool's trick.

There was a real treat on television for Mollie. On a local channel the weatherman Roy Leep had a "Weather Dog." The real live dog's name was Scud which means a low flying cloud. Every evening Scud was dressed in clothes befitting the next day's forecast. Mollie liked what she was seeing so far in Tampa Bay.

The first day of work was an eye opener. Mollie was told that the hospital would be fined a million dollars by the government if a certain amount of patients and families were not treated for free. Mollie was expected to work evenings and Saturdays to meet this quota by July first. She had three months.

As she worked hard, the other two social workers informed her that another social worker had been offered Mollie's position before Mollie. She had turned it down, but changed her mind. It was too late because Mollie had already accepted the job. The woman apparently held a high social work office in Florida. Mollie sensed the other two social workers' disappointment.

Mollie did family therapy at this hospital. Two parents of a twenty-one year old met with Mollie. They told her that their son had packed his clothes and told them that, "I am going to go and meet Jesus."

Not knowing for sure whether they knew that their son was delusional, Mollie explored the issue more. The parents finally raised their voices with conviction and said, "Jesus is coming! Jesus is coming!"

At that precise moment there was a knock on the door. Mollie answered it. No one was there---not even Jesus.

One thing that Mollie didn't like about the area was the smell of the drinking water and the shower water. It was foul. Mollie mentioned this to someone at work and they acknowledged it was a problem. She reframed it by saying, "We all stink the same way."

July first arrived and the quota had been met. The hospital had been spared a million dollars. Mollie was proud of herself.

Bastille Day arrived. Mollie was called into the Director of Nursing's office and fired. No reason was given. Mollie suspected that the other social worker who had originally been offered the job took her place. That social worker had visited a couple weeks earlier for no apparent reason that Mollie could see at the time.

Before she left the nurse's office, the nurse said to Mollie, "Don't you want to punch me?" Mollie was too stunned to take her up on the offer. She walked out with her head down.

The next day Mollie went to Indian Rocks Beach on the Gulf of Mexico which was a few miles from where she lived. She sat on the beach hoping to see some dolphins. Mollie believed seeing dolphins was good luck. She saw none. Even so, the beach was a refuge. It brought back the comfort of John's Sanwadoon.

Mollie stayed unemployed for the next four months except for a short month of temporary work. She was finally hired by a private psychiatric hospital in Tampa. That meant she had to drive across the Howard Frankland Bridge every day much to her pleasure. Being by the water was soothing whether by the beach or by it in the car.

Dr. Minton had referred Mollie to a psychiatrist in Tampa for Mollie to follow up with for her treatment. She wasn't wild about him even though he was personally acquainted with Dr. Minton. One time he remarked about the disadvantage he felt.

He said, "You want me to wear a wig and a dress and be Dr. Minton."

Mollie didn't think he really understood. After all, she had seen Dr. Minton for nineteen years by this time.

The job at the psychiatric hospital was much to Mollie's liking. She enjoyed inpatient work and she further honed her group therapy skills.

One day two new female psychiatrists started there. They both looked to be six feet tall although later the one psychiatrist admitted to being five foot ten.

Little did Mollie know how this physician would later loom in her life.

CHAPTER 16

What Mollie did not like was that the hospital began having financial trouble after Mollie worked there for a year. Employees were being laid off in droves. It turned out that there had been embezzlement going on at the top of the company.

Because she was used to being fired for no reason, Mollie decided to go job hunting. She quickly found one several miles from her apartment. The job was as a child therapist at a nonprofit agency.

Mollie quickly felt like a dolphin out of water there. No one gave her an overture of friendliness. The third day she got her hopes up. Another therapist appeared at Mollie's office door and asked, "Do you have plans for lunch?"

Mollie answered expectantly. "No."

The therapist delivered the kicker. "Good. You can cover the phones while we go out."

Mollie wanted to heave a salami sandwich at her. Instead, she answered the phones with a funny voice because of the lump in her throat.

Then she found a part-time job on a psychiatric unit in a general hospital. Mollie found that keeping busy like this did ease the sting of rejection.

At the hospital she ran into a psychiatrist she had worked with at the other hospital that she left in Tampa. He offered her a full-time job as a Director for a partial hospitalization program. It would mean a minimum of an one hour commute one way. It would mean quitting a job she disliked. It meant that Mollie accepted the position.

Mollie had an appointment with the doctor that wanted to wear a wig for Mollie. The patient that left before Mollie's appointment looked angry as she exited. Mollie wondered what that was all about.

She found out. Mollie described some side effects of the medication she was on. The psychiatrist stood up and started feeling up Mollie's arm. Something wasn't right. Her side effects had nothing to do with her arm. She left and never went back.

Mollie had to decide upon a new psychiatrist. It would be a tall order, but she made an appointment with Dr. Mary Silos.

The first appointment was difficult. It wasn't easy to disclose once again to someone who was virtually a stranger. Mollie had felt she had been burned by this last yahoo of a psychiatrist so she had trust issues.

Like Dr. Minton Dr. Silos was patient and kind. She allowed Mollie to warm up to her gradually. At first, all Mollie would say was, "This is hard. This is hard."

Mollie loved her new job. She picked out the furniture and the decor. Her Activities Director was the best and had what seemed like an unlimited budget with which to work. Mollie had a workable number of patients to work with during the daytime hours that they were there. The ten or so patients bonded well and the program was a success. The doctor was next door and saw the patients at least a couple of times a week.

As far as Mollie's mental health she was stabilized. It had been close to twenty years since she had been psychiatrically hospitalized.

Being in charge of the program let Mollie not feel rejection. She tried to make everyone feel included.

Joan, the Activities Director, even invited Mollie for Thanksgiving at her parent's home. Mollie went and met Joan's mother at the door. Her mother was wearing a small bottle around her neck. The fad at the time was wearing bubbles with a wand around the neck. Mollie made polite conversation.

"What is in your bottle?"

"Oh, those are my toenails."

Mollie refrained from asking any more questions. She definitely did not ask what was in the stuffing.

Around this time Mollie decided she wanted to get a puppy. She thought it would be a good addition to the partial hospitalization program. Mollie was prone to poodles because of growing up with Lassie. It would be a joy to have a dog around again. As a friend of hers once told her, "Having a dog is like having a perpetual three year old."

The program psychiatrist's secretary knew of a poodle breeder whose dog had just had puppies. They were miniatures just like Mollie desired. She selected a little male apricot puff ball with white paws and a white chest. He was a quick study.

Mollie attempted over a number of weeks to talk to the program psychiatrist. She thought she had better obtain his blessing about bringing a puppy to the program. He was always busy and could not talk to her. They never did discuss it.

The puppy was named Happie. He was housebroken in three days and galloped up a flight of twenty steps to Mollie's apartment once he grew a little bigger.

He behaved well at the program. The patients loved to pet him and Happie instinctively comforted patients as they cried.

Mollie made sure she held Happie in her lap when the psychiatrist was in her office. It was just insurance so there was no uncomfortable confrontation between the two of them.

Then Happie started to act out. Mollie had penned him in the kitchen when she went out. On her return the paper towels had been knocked down from the counter and strewn so that they covered the entire floor. That wouldn't have been so bad, but Happie had peed all over them.

Happie began snapping too. He nipped Bud's hand when he visited.

A friend of Mollie's came over and flipped off her sandals. Happie went over and claimed one as his own by peeing on it.

Mollie took Happie to doggy day care. It was reported that he was having accidents there.

Even though things were not ideal, Mollie met a man whom she found attractive. He was the brother of a woman who ran a boarding home for some of Mollie's patients. Tim was a former minor league baseball player. He was handsome with his jet black hair and blue eyes. His easygoing manner appealed to Mollie. Tim visited the program a couple of times and he and Mollie kept busy flirting with each other.

Mollie was happy; Happie wasn't. He seemed disoriented at times and staggered. He would not respond to his name when he was like this. Mollie took him to the vet and Happie was diagnosed with a seizure disorder. He was put on medication.

Mollie was able to take a vacation from work. Before she left, she had to orient the new Nursing Director. She was the wife of a psychiatrist and perkier than coffee. One day she followed Mollie into a meeting she had scheduled with someone outside the program. Mollie told her this meeting was not for her.

"I just want to follow you around and learn everything you do."

When Mollie returned from vacation, she found out that this nurse had moved into her office and taken over her desk. Mollie knew she was in trouble. She didn't know what to do.

She kept her eye on this nurse and didn't like what she saw. The woman barely worked. One day Mollie overheard her talking to the program psychiatrist. They were discussing how the nurse's husband and the program psychiatrist could do business together.

The day of reckoning arrived. Mollie was doing a group and in the background she could see and hear the nurse gabbing away with the secretary. After the group Mollie asked her to take the blood pressure of a 300 pound patient who wasn't feeling well. The nurse refused. She told Mollie to do it. There was no good reason that the nurse couldn't do it.

The nurse played hysterical. She raised her voice and ran out the front door after saying, "I quit."

Mollie found her next door at the psychiatrist's office. He was not in yet. Because the nurse had quit, Mollie asked her for her keys. She refused as she cried. She was putting on quite a show for the office staff. Mollie did not know what the nurse had told them.

Mollie returned to the program and proceeded to run it without the useless nurse. The psychiatrist did not see it that way. He called Mollie into his office and would not listen to her side of the story. He fired her and put in the final sting by saying "With my brains and my education you will never catch me."

He may have had those things going for him, but he lacked any scintilla of class. The man picked his nose like he was digging for gold.

Feeling defeated again Mollie drove home. She had done excellent work for the more than a year that she had worked there. Now what?

The first thing she did was file for unemployment compensation. The psychiatrist contested it. They squared off at a hearing where the doctor heard Mollie's side of the story for the first time.

Mollie won. The hearing officer found the psychiatrist's testimony to be "incompetent." Mollie had won the battle, but lost the war.

Mollie loved her jobs, but her coworkers did not seem to love her. This was a pattern which repeated itself over and over. Mollie had sixteen jobs in fifteen years and was fired from six of them and three of them folded on their own. If nothing else, Mollie was flexible.

At first Mollie blamed herself for being fired so frequently. When she examined the whole situation, it became clear that the pathology of the work place was like a boa constrictor that squeezed her out while keeping the feisty rats around for its emotional sustenance. Mollie was probably the hardest worker that was ever fired from these places.

Part of the problem with Mollie was that she was an excellent worker and stood out in contrast to others. She was bright, competent, confident, and a visible threat to anyone with eyes. Usually she was shot down within a year. It was distressing to Mollie, but she always managed to find something else even though it would not be anything near to being a dream job.

Mollie found a job within two months. She had to travel to four nursing homes in three counties and do individual assessments as well as individual counseling with the elderly. She also did group therapy with the elderly despite frequent resistance from them. These folks had managed to weather their lives up until now without much interference. Eighty and ninety year olds had to have good coping skills to sidle up to their birthday cupcakes at this point. Their need for psychotherapy was questionable.

At the start of this job Mollie started doing something else. She began cutting back on her Lithium™. No longer taking a therapeutic dose meant she was playing mental health roulette.

Mollie also stopped Happie's seizure medication. It didn't seem to be making any difference.

The third thing Mollie did in this trifecta of bad judgment was contacting Tim. He came over one evening.

They made out and then spooned on the bed. Their bodies were cradled together in coziness. The next morning Mollie felt that she was in love with this man. The only thing they had in common was their love of baseball and their coloring of black hair and blue eyes. He was an uneducated farm boy. Maybe the lack of Lithium™ was clouding Mollie's common sense.

A week later Tim asked her to marry him. Mollie said yes.

Mollie was wired with energy. She wasn't sleeping well. It was easy for her to attribute this to being in love.

Mollie's parents visited for the winter and stayed with Mollie. They were flabbergasted that Mollie was getting married since they did not know she was dating anyone.

They met Tim over a golf game and did not hide their disdain from Mollie afterwards. The apartment was filled with tension and conflict.

Then Bud and Helen did an about face. They wanted Mollie to invite Tim over for dinner. Mollie suspected this was some sort of test. She invited Tim and the dinner date was set.

The special night arrived. Helen had made a chicken and rice dish which was out of this galaxy. The appointed time for dinner came and went. No Tim. There was no word from Tim. After a long wait Mollie called him. There was no answer. He never showed up.

Mollie did reach him. It was past midnight and he was past the legal limit of intoxication. That was the end of Mollie's engagement, but not of her rejection issues.

A month and a half later Mollie was on her bed while talking on the phone with a friend (the one whose sandal Happie urinated on). Happie was a week shy of his first birthday. He hopped up on the bed to be next to Mollie.

Mollie reached out to pet him. Happie turned and bit Mollie. He growled as Mollie jumped off the bed. Happie lunged and showed his teeth. He peeled off some of the skin on Mollie's hands as he attacked. He would not stop. He looked crazed.

Mollie was able to get him on the floor and rolled him on his side. He looked wild and tried to snap at her. Mollie looked up and prayed, "God, forgive me." With that she stopped the violence by strangling her beloved dog with her hands.

In six months Mollie had lost her dog, her fiance, and her job. They were heartbreaking losses.

The next day Mollie contacted Dr. Silos. She determined that Mollie needed to be psychiatrically hospitalized. Mollie drove herself there.

Mollie slept in a chair in her hospital room. She could not bring herself to sleep in a bed because of where the attack took place. She felt wretched. Killing your own dog was like a "Thou Shalt Not" if there were an Eleventh Commandment.

There was something else besides the bed in the hospital room that bothered her. The carpeting was like what was in her family's living room in Kent. Mollie took the thought a step further and concluded it was also the same type of carpet that Eisenhower had in The White House.

Mollie noticed the dressers were of the same type that John had at Sanwadoon. Both the carpet and dressers may have been coincidences, but they paralleled instances of reality in Mollie's frame of reference. She coined the phrase "parallel coincidences" for these things.

At this point Mollie strongly believed her father had something to do with the trio of assassinations in the sixties: JFK, Martin Luther King Jr., and Robert F. Kennedy. She had no idea where these inklings began. With clues like possibly moving to Dallas where the assassination happened and the Texas State Book Depository connection where Oswald fired the fatal shots and where her father's company stored books fueled Mollie's suspicions. She wondered about the black walnut that Bud had given her from when he was at the LBJ ranch. The other thing she was bothered about was the photo of Lee Harvey Oswald being shot by Jack Ruby. The photo looked staged with reporters parted like the Red Sea for an anticipated photo opportunity. Also Lee Harvey Oswald looked like her grandpa's neighbor. His first name was Lee.

Was this Mollie's imagination, her mental illness, the suppressed truth or partly Mollie's intuition? Mollie always had a strong intuition. Years of assimilating this odd stuff made her mind percolate.

Mollie was known to be extremely observant. She read once that intuition is cultivated by having a keen sense of observation. Mollie's power of observation was right up there with her keen size appetite.

Dr. Minton used to ask Mollie, "How do you feel?" That simple question might have caused Mollie's intuition to proliferate. She was observing her feelings about what she observed.

Years later Mollie read an article about those who have strong intuition. Dogs are thought to be smarter than cats for just this reason. Dogs keep up with every mood and move in the home and can keep tabs on everything. They have keen powers of intuition and can put together the puzzle pieces by piecing together these observations. Mollie had a dog one time that became excited every time that Mollie brushed her hair. The dog knew this meant they were going for a walk.

Mollie knew more about dogs than some of her feelings. For instance, she knew that dogs supposedly did not have tails until they were domesticated by humans. She also knew that the dogs' nearest relative going way back in time was the bear.

With too much information to sort out Mollie knew her life was very unusual from most of the population. Mollie really did not know with 100% conviction whether she was delusional or not due to her extra sensory perception. One thing was for sure. It was 100% weird.

Her intuition and strong sense of a kind of extra sensory perception or psychic phenomena had been experienced by any number of people. She had a kind of energy force where she would pile hospital charts on a chair. Ten minutes later they would leap onto the floor.

Another time she had worn an angel pin on her blazer and while speaking with her supervisor, it went SPRONGGGG. Mollie asked what happened and her boss said, "Your pin just flew into that corner." That corner was a good four feet away.

Sometimes this strange force manifested itself in other fun ways. Because Mollie grew up with two brothers and a father who favored basketball, any crumpled up napkin became a basketball at the dinner table. Any drinking glass became a basketball hoop. Mollie could whisk impossible shots into the drinking glasses with the greatest of ease and with no forethought. Bud would marvel and laugh as he saw Mollie do this.

"You're unconscious!" he exclaimed.

She could roll dice unconsciously too. Mollie was competitive and had taught many people how to play backgammon. More times than not she could roll doubles when needed. As she shook the dice, there was a pulse of energy she felt in her hands. It was a tingling sensation. She knew it was odd. It couldn't be explained by usual thought. Mollie kept rolling strong.

Mollie wondered whether it was a type of supernatural force. After all, her mother told her, "Your guardian angels work overtime."

Mollie suspected they played overtime with her too. Strange things kept happening to Mollie like some sort of cosmic practical jokes. For example, there was the antique clock stored in the attic when Mollie lived with her parents. At 2 A.M. the clock gonged a couple of times. Mollie's bedroom was directly underneath the clock's attic location.

Years later Bud and Helen took the clock in to be repaired. The clock doc said that all of the wires in the clock's back were hopelessly crossed so that nothing worked. There was no reason it should have gonged in the middle of the night.

Another thing that happened to Mollie was a lamp would come on for no reason in her presence. In department stores one or two clothing racks would crash to the floor next to Mollie without Mollie so much as touching them.

Mollie's imagination was another factor. In the hospital this time her room was next to the nursing station. She heard the psychiatrists come in and ask, "Is the baby here?" For some reason Mollie thought they were talking about her, but ceded to herself that maybe they were talking about an expectant staff member.

Another time she happened into the middle of a conversation between a nurse and a tech. They did not see her at first. The nurse was telling the tech, "When you find out who she is, let me know." They abruptly ended their conversation when they saw Mollie. Mollie was no narcissist. Her gut feeling told her that this was about her.

As far as Mollie was concerned, going into the hospital was somewhat of a joke. Patients were told that they were "safe" in the hospital. How was that? The patients were so safe that they were locked in. Medication was forced. If medication were refused, then it was given by injection. There was no rest. Others were screaming all the live long day. Patients went into other patients' rooms and stole anything. It was nothing short of psychological warfare.

Patients were turned into sleeping fish because they were loaded to the gills with pills. A patient would see the snap judgment psychiatrist for maybe fifteen minutes a day or less. The mouth of a patient began to pucker up in a parched fashion as a side effect of medication. Weight gain was usually another side effect of medication.

Out of this environment Mollie managed to regain some of her sanity. She learned not to talk about anything that might undermine her credibility. She was released after close to two weeks of being in the hospital.

Mollie was obsessed with UFOs and aliens. She read about Roswell, New Mexico and how a baby alien was found at the site of an UFO crash there in 1947. Mollie suspected she might be that baby. After all, people were inquiring about whether the baby was there in the hospital. Even though she was born in 1952, maybe that was a made up date.

For some reason Mollie was obsessed with Amelia Earhart too. She had bought a book about her years earlier. Besides reading this one she checked out others from the library. Mollie thought that maybe she was related to Amelia. She had thought about writing a screenplay about how a social worker discovers Amelia in a nursing home.

Prior to the nurse who set up Mollie's firing from the partial hospitalization program, there was another nurse. She was a seventy-two year old sprite. One of her hobbies was looking at real estate. She sneaked into houses that were for sale to look at them. She told Mollie that one time she was able to crawl into the small window of the house of the opera singer Beverly Sills. Then she and her friend made a ridiculously low offer on the Tampa home.

Reportedly Ms. Sills lost her voice for a week when that offer came in.

The nurse told Mollie that her former husband had been a Three Star Colonel in the Air Force. Mollie asked if she knew anything about UFOs. The nurse said her former husband had told her that there were "beings" that were found in the desert. Sometime after this the nurse freaked out and accused Mollie of "picking my brain." She resigned shortly after that.

Mollie began seeing Dr. Silos intensively after her release from the hospital. She began talking about UFOs and Amelia Earhart.

Mollie wasn't sure whether she was actually one handle short of being a teacup. Her self doubts doubted themselves. She had spent twenty-eight years of her life in therapy. Whereas Woody Allen had been in analysis for decades, he was considered a creative genius. Mollie was a pain in the butt bipolar.

Mollie had always tried to live her life to the fullest and fulfill goals, yet even her goals had been tainted by her mental illness. She knew there was no way in San Jose that she could be elected President of the United States. Scratch that off her lottery ticket. Being an astronaut was out of the question too unless there was a study on spaciness in space. On the other hand she didn't want to aim too low such as becoming a turnip farmer although on many days she felt as if she had dropped off the turnip truck.

Often times, Mollie felt completely vegged out like a limp carrot because of her medication. There were days when Mollie woke up to the fact that most people would have thought they were dead if they had been in her bunny slippers. Mollie had to constantly fight against this half dazed, half asleep condition. It was like being on a slow motion hamster treadmill. She had to take more medication when she got up in the morning after taking some the night before. Mollie never knew whether she was getting up or going to bed.

Although Mollie seemed robbed of her dreams, she lived by two specific credos. One was, "I'd rather teach one bird how to sing than teach ten thousand stars how not to dance." That was from ee cummings.

Her other credo was from Thoreau. "To affect the quality of the day is the highest of arts."

Mollie felt she was affecting other's lives, but wasn't sure how. It was a mystery she wanted to unravel in therapy. She thought Dr. Silos could help her get to the bottom of all the weird stuff accumulated in the wake of Mollie's psyche.

CHAPTER 17

Dr. Silos was tough. She was rotund and usually there was a filled candy dish in the office to maintain her shape. Mollie was particularly fond of the butterscotch ones.

Just greeting this psychiatrist at her office taunted Mollie's self-esteem not to drop lower. Dr. Silos's piercing eyes and great intellect with her height towered over Mollie. She lunged when she walked and always led the way to her office at a brisk pace as if the ice cream were melting. Of course there was no ice cream. If there had been, its flavor would have been "Urgency."

Mollie took her place on the sofa which sunk lower than Mollie wanted to go. As one of Mollie's elderly clients once told her, "Overstuffed isn't as comfortable as it used to be."

Dr. Silos had a wicked wit. One time Mollie noted that Dr. Silos and Dr. Pudgy had the same layout of furniture. Both of them had graduated from Case Western Reserve. Dr. Silos was quick.

"We took the same furniture arranging class."

Mollie thought it was interesting that Dr. Silos was originally from Ohio. She had taught at Kent State. Mollie wondered if this were a coincidence.

Mollie had heard the adage that neurotics dream of castles in the air, psychotics build castles in the air, and psychiatrists collect the rent. Dr. Silos was no nonsense and did not allow her patients to even build a moat in the air.

Mollie had asked her not to "sugar coat" anything. Dr. Silos adhered to that. She was a blunt instrument when it came to giving feedback or confronting Mollie. The doctor tended to shock Mollie into silence as Mollie had to integrate what was just said. She knew that Dr. Silos had a softer side too. She liked to garden and Mollie thought that the doc couldn't be that mean and have her flowers survive.

Dr. Silos encouraged Mollie to use her gifts of humor, writing, and creativity. Mollie was stuck in some kind of creativity block and Dr. Silos gently nudged her to write without critiquing herself as she forged ahead. Occasionally Mollie would bring a joke to the session and was heartened when Dr. Silos would smile or even laugh.

Mollie told her one story that made Dr. Silos beam.

"An elderly man was waiting at a bus stop. A young punk came up to wait too. He had a bright red, yellow, and iridescent green Mohawk. The elderly man looked at him.

The punk got upset. 'What are you looking at, old man?'

The older man answered. 'I once had an affair with a parrot and I thought you might be my long lost son.'"

"That's a keeper," said Dr. Silos.

Mollie liked to make others laugh as much as she liked to laugh. Laughing helped suspend her stress level for a few moments and gave her a sense of relief. It wasn't a form of denial or a defense mechanism. It just felt good.

There were oddities that Mollie didn't talk about. A colleague at the first psychiatric hospital she worked at told Mollie, "I'm in denial."

"I'm going to go into denial too," said Mollie.

The colleague said, "No, you can't do that."

This was the same colleague who attended a patient sing-a-long with Mollie. Afterwards she told Mollie, "It's a good thing you are a therapist."

Fishing for a compliment Mollie asked, "Why?"

"Because you sure can't sing..."

The first couple of years were rough going with Dr. Silos. Mollie skirted issues as she led up to some sort of trust level with the doctor.

Mollie began to bring up the subject of aliens and UFOs. This isn't normally a great idea to bring up to a shrink because of it being considered delusional. Dr. Silos instructed Mollie not to watch "The X Files" on TV. Mollie was curious, but obeyed her admonition about this program about space aliens. However, she did watch "The Autopsy of an Alien" and she did not know whether to believe it was real or not.

Mollie charged ahead with this trust that was being established. She related the story about her nurse employee whose Three Star Colonel Air Force husband talked about the "beings" at Roswell, New Mexico in 1947.

She began reading even more about UFOs and space aliens. Mollie learned that aliens liked Gregorian chants and strawberry ice cream.

Mollie mentioned this to Dr. Silos in their next session. The doctor's response threw her for a loop-dee-loo.

Dr. Silos said, "Strawberry ice cream is my favorite and I like Gregorian chants."

Mollie missed her opportunity to ask her if she were an alien. Her suspicions were aroused, but Dr. Silos was too tall to be a "being." According to what Mollie had read, space beings were supposedly as short as children.

Mollie's boss at the time gave her more to consider. Knowing her boss's father was a Three Star General in the Air Force, Mollie casually mentioned something totally out of context as they chatted one day.

"I've heard that there are "beings" warehoused at Wright-Patterson Air Force Base."

Mollie's boss sighed. "Yes, there are."

It shook Mollie up. Two separate parties connected to the Air Force had confirmed her belief that there were space beings that had visited earth.

Another couple of factors also shook Mollie up. Helen had told Mollie that she and Bud were going to go to a psychiatrist. They wanted to go to Dr. Minton, but she told them she was retiring.

Mollie felt compelled to tell her boss about this bit of information. Her boss sat back and reflected.

"I wonder what that is about."

Mollie wondered about it too. She asked her parents whether it had anything to do with her. They assured her that it didn't.

After their session with a shrink that Dr. Minton had referred them to see, Mollie talked with Dr. Minton by phone. She told Dr. Minton about John's sail boat. Mollie heard the controlled excitement in Dr. Minton's voice.

"Where is is?"

Mollie told her it had been covered up with sand at the bottom of the bluff's stairs at Sanwadoon. Later in their conversation Mollie mentioned that she wanted to write a book.

Dr. Minton's response was interesting. "You can write volumes."

Mollie wondered about this odd response. It dawned on her years later that maybe Dr. Minton knew about her father. Maybe that's what Mollie's parents wanted to talk to the shrink about and that shrink told Dr. Minton about Bud's involvement in JFK's assassination.

After that, Mollie barely had any contact with Dr. Minton. They did exchange birthday and Christmas cards.

Mollie could not stand being in the apartment where Happie had attacked her. She moved one town south to St. Petersburg, Florida.

By this time she had confided in Dr. Silos about how she believed her father had been part of the plan to kill Kennedy. Dr. Silos listened intently without any obvious reaction.

During one session there was a huge crashing sound from the floor above them. Dr. Silos was quick to gloss over it.

"That has nothing to do with you.'

Mollie countered with anger and fright. "How do YOU know?"

In one of her first sessions with Dr. Silos Mollie confided that she believed Richard Nixon was her real father. Dr. Silos was most impressed because that evening it was all over the news that Nixon had sustained a stroke. No one was really following his life at this moment in time because his grace had not shed on thee for many years. Nixon could not do anything right. He massacred the peace sign. Maybe not though. He probably meant it as a victory sign. Mollie knew he liked dogs, so she overlooked the more obvious pathological cues oozing from this former President.

Mollie was ashamed about a dream she had at one time about Nixon. She and Nixon were perched on the top of the backseat of a convertible with its top down. They were in a parade going downtown Chicago on Lakeshore Drive with ticker tape swirling around and the crowd trying to lurch through the police barriers. It hadn't dawned on

Mollie that this might have been more of a riot than anything else.

This wasn't the type of stuff you talk about over a Thanksgiving dinner and Mollie did not divulge the dream to Dr. Silos. Anyway, Mollie realized that the dream was probably triggered by a Nixon campaign photo she was given in the fourth grade. Being an enthused Nixon advocate was an indicator of her common sense at that time. As an adult she sublimated all that political fervor into collecting political campaign buttons.

Mollie brought up to Dr. Silos about how she wanted to delve into what others considered her delusions yet she did not. Dr. Silos whipped her head up and questioned this.

"Do you really want to do this?"

"Yes," answered Mollie even though she was not sure what all would be involved. At this point she trusted Dr. Silos.

Mollie indulged this trust one night. One of her pastimes was to read magazines and newspapers. After one hospitalization she was flipping through Good Housekeeping (goodness knows that Mollie could use help in that regard). Being a person like the majority of the population she tended to notice visual things. This meant her attention was drawn to the photos. She studied the picture of Rosemary Kennedy who was the daughter of Joseph P. and Rose Kennedy. Mollie couldn't get over how she resembled Mollie's mother Helen.

Mollie promptly telephoned Dr. Silos. When Dr. Silos called back, Mollie asked her, "Is my mother Rosemary Kennedy?"

Dr. Silos raised her voice like she was upset. "I DON'T KNOW!" she barked out.

From that Mollie extrapolated. She didn't tell Dr. Silos this meant she might be Rosemary's baby like in the movie. This would mean she had an evil essence.

Not long after this Mollie felt she had a confirmation of her evil essence. The shocker came when she went to work at one of her assigned nursing homes. She went into a room to see an elderly woman who was suffering from depression. Mollie was jolted by the declaration of her patient's roommate who yelled out, "That's Hitler's daughter! That's Hitler's daughter."

Mollie mused over the accusation. She knew she wasn't Hitler's daughter, but maybe she was Hitler's granddaughter. She was the pariah of all pariahs.

Mollie's identity felt jumbled up. At least twice Dr. Silos extended her right arm with her right hand clenched into a fist as she thumped her heart and asked the question.

"Who are you?" Her booming voice ricocheted around the room.

Mollie always answered the same way. "Mollie."

What bothered her was what she had read about Patty Hearst being deprogrammed after being rescued from her captors. Her deprogrammer had done the same gesture and asked the same question in her intervention.

Another confusing aspect of Mollie's identity was her name. Mollie remembered again how she was named after a little girl whom she and her older brother had played together. It did not make sense. Mollie had not been born yet and her brother was barely two when she was born. Mollie began playing around with the letters in her name.

All she had to do was space the letters in order in her name. MO meant "Modus Operandi." LLIES meant "Lies." KIL equalled "Kill." SS meant the German SS.

MO=lies kill SS. It was her name in sequence. This was further proof to her that she might be related to Hitler. She wasn't sure how everything tied together.

Being Rosemary's baby might be the Kennedy curse she kept hearing about. Being Hitler's granddaughter was a curse too. The gene cesspool needed to be addressed instead of being such a secret. Her father may have had something to do with the Kennedy assassination. Mollie knew this was dangerous territory and that she might be the only one paying for it. No one needed any more tragedies. Maybe therapy had been a test for her all of these years. Maybe therapy was a way for Mollie to figure stuff out and a way to extend forgiveness as well as to decide how to move on without anymore games. The truth could have serious consequences for any number of people. What reverberated constantly in her brain was that phrase, "You are as sick as your secrets."

Dr. Silos asked Mollie several times about why she was telling her about her father's possible involvement in the Kennedy assassination. Part of it was being as sick as your secrets. The other part was that Mollie believed Dr. Silos could do something about it.

That's what caught Mollie off guard when Dr. Silos asked her, "What about the truth?"

Mollie was stunned about that because in her reality she was telling the truth. She wasn't sure that Dr. Silos wanted the truth or simply wanted information from Mollie.

Shortly after Mollie was accused of being Hitler's daughter, she was hospitalized again by Dr. Silos.

A couple of oddities happened while Mollie was there. One night she entered the dayroom where a woman was trying to sleep. Mollie asked if she could sit on the sofa. The woman said it was all right. Not long after this the woman rushed out of the room exclaiming, "I remember! I remember!"

The next day Mollie approached a staff member to talk. He was on the phone and Mollie heard him say, "The Amazing Mollie did it again!" Mollie believed it had to do with the woman who rushed out of the dayroom the night before this.

Helen and Bud drove down to Florida from Illinois for a family session. Mollie was quite wound up for it. During the session she asked her father if she were Princess Diana.

"Why do you ask that?" he said.

"Because you used to tell me to get off of my high horse."

Despite the ineffective family session Mollie was discharged from the hospital a couple of weeks later.

Dr. Silos and Mollie had regular therapy sessions. They talked about everything. Mollie was sure that Bud was not her father. The photocopied birth certificate from Ohio was not convincing enough for Mollie.

Mollie revealed how she thought she was related to Amelia Earhart. She also disclosed how she was such "a fool" and wondered how April Fool's Day got started. Dr. Silos suggested that she research it in the library.

Mollie did. One reference said that it was Air Force Day and had to be designated by the President. Mollie took this to mean that because of her birthdate April Fool's Day that she had something to do with the Air Force, Amelia Earhart, and aliens.

For one session Mollie burst into Dr. Silo's office and threw herself into a chair. She felt like she was in a panic and out of her mouth came words she had never had before nor thought to utter.

"I'm a burnt out star and I need to go back to the mother ship to refuel."

Dr. Silos calmed her down by the end of the session. Dr. Silos suggested that Mollie attend The Space Cadet Academy. Mollie said she would think about it.

Mollie came in for her next session and told Dr. Silos that she would like to attend The Space Cadet Academy. Dr. Silos swept it aside.

"That was a mistake." It was most likely her sense of humor.

Mollie didn't challenge her. She did challenge Dr. Silos on something else. She noticed that Dr. Silos appeared different from week to week. Her height seemed to vary. Her patience fluctuated from time to time. Her facial features were often quite different.

Mollie would ask her, "Do you have a double?"

Dr. Silos always had the same answer. "What do you mean?"

Mollie took that as a "yes."

Mollie did not confide everything. Mollie's initials spelled "SAM" backwards because her middle name was Ann. She was listening to the radio one day as she rested. The radio had a woman on who was excitedly saying, "We've found SAM!" At the same time there were the sounds of jet planes in the air. Mollie lived relatively close to MacDill Air Force Base. She knew this was about her, but deliberately went on without any sense of letting on what was going on with her.

Mollie was convinced that her family was keeping many secrets. She questioned whether these secrets were being covered up with white lies and being kept to protect her. She had come to the conclusion that maybe her parents had been reconfigured and were incapable of remembering vital facts. Mollie herself often had a sensation of a steel door swinging shut which felt like a memory slamming shut.

Mollie told Dr. Silos, "There's something I feel like I need to remember, but I can't remember what it is."

Dr. Silos's response was, "You will remember everything."

Mollie wondered about whether this would happen since she had electro-convulsive treatment. "Since I had ECT, will that mean some of my memory won't come back?"

Dr. Silos stared into Mollie's eyes with her own hazel ones. "I will have to check with my colleagues in Boston."

The Kennedys were connected with Boston. Was Dr. Silos connected with the Kennedys?

Mollie remembered a weird incident when Dr. Minton had her hospitalized for the second time in Chicago. During one long afternoon Mollie noticed that most of the patients and a good many of the staff were riveted to the television in the dayroom. Mollie ambled over to see what they were watching.

It caught her off guard and she told herself that it couldn't be. Denial, delusional, or reality? Paper, scissors, or rock? This was rock solid, but there was no one Mollie could turn to at the moment who wouldn't turn it around to her being sick.

What was on TV was Mollie as a little girl of maybe eight years old. She was wearing a red, white, and blue striped outfit which was a favorite pick of her mother. Mollie was trying to catch up with her older brother in a wooded area circling Silver Lake in Ohio. She was huffing and puffing with the determination that was being honed for coping with future stress in her life.

Mollie reflected. Whenever there was a contest at work to identify baby pictures, Mollie's baby photo was always recognized. No wondering about it now. She was having exposure to the public that she obviously hadn't been aware of at all.

She did think about why it was so vital to keep her in the dark. Were all the bizarre excerpts of her life a way that others were giving her hints about something she should remember?

Mollie was painfully aware that her credibility was zero to the nth degree because of her flareups from time to time of her bipolar disorder. Her bipolar disorder was like an outbreak of pimples yet the acne does not usually change the ultimate facial structure. It cleared up. What she wondered about didn't seem to clear up.

Mollie was hesitant to talk about things like she saw on the TV that day in the hospital. Anything she said could be used against her in the name of symptomatology. She was like the proverbial pink elephant to whom no one would talk to her about this stuff.

She felt a compulsion to confide in Dr. Silos. She had three decades of psychiatric intervention (interference?) by this time. With her head shrunk that much, Mollie's brain was probably the size of an apricot pit.

Someone had pointed out to her that therapy is like peeling back an onion one layer at a time. This is the process of discovery and insight. Yet, at the finish of peeling an onion is the sad fact that there is nothing left at the end. Tears have been shed. The onion's pungent odor has been chewed away. It has been totally used. Every day that went by meant that Mollie was getting closer to the intelligence and emotional quotient of a Vidalia.

Mollie took one last stab at disclosing to Dr. Silos. After all, Dr. Silos had already told Mollie that she was "eccentric."

She brought in the black walnut from the LBJ Ranch that her father had given her. With uncharacteristic boldness Mollie flung the nut onto Dr. Silo's desk and taunted her.

"Analyze this!"

At that precise moment laughter erupted from the office next door. Mollie wondered about whether they had been monitoring their session. Neither Mollie nor Dr. Silos addressed the issue.

Mollie was in treatment with Dr. Silos for nine years until Dr. Silos announced that she was moving out of state. Mollie was crushed. She had entrusted so many secrets to Dr. Silos and her bipolar illness had been kept in check. No more Dr. Silos. No more confiding. It was too painful to begin all over again.

The onion was peeled.

CHAPTER 18

Mollie began recognizing the strangeness in her family of origin. For instance, Mollie's older brother had taught her the love of baseball when she was five years old. They both collected baseball cards. In her mid-twenties Mollie found her box of cards in the attic. Whitey Ford, Ted Williams, Roger Maris, and Mickey Mantle were all there. The collectible baseball card craze was beginning, so Mollie gave her cards to Matt. Mollie did not realize until later that she had gifted him with a small fortune.

Twenty years later Matt gave Mollie one baseball card of a player whom he said was a distant relative . He had not played notoriously in The Major Leagues way back when. It was autographed. Mollie noticed it was Matt's handwriting. She said something to him about it and Matt moaned. He sounded like a sick cow.

When Matt was in his forties, there was another strange incident. They were riding in the car with their parents. Suddenly and out of context Matt dramatically exclaimed, "I was tricked! I will never trust anyone again!" Mollie never did find out what that was all about.

Mark had a different quirk. He had worked on the graveyard shift as a cop. He told the story of seeing an UFO in the Kansas skies in the dark of night. He radioed another cop on patrol across town. Both of them turned their searchlights on it. Whatever it was, it zoomed away faster than they could issue a speeding ticket.

Mark ultimately finished law school and interviewed with the FBI. He called Bud because he was concerned that something he didn't know about would show up on his background check.

Bud was reassuring. "With all the overweight people in our family, they won't find any skeletons in the closet."

Mark became a FBI Special Agent. After a few years of him capturing significant culprits, Mollie brought up the subject of the Kansas UFO that Mark had spotted years ago. Mark denied that it ever happened.

There were too many fishy things swirling around in Mollie's goldfish bowl of life. To her one group of people seemed to think they were protecting Mollie from "the truth" by hiding it from her. The other group of people seemed to want to help Mollie remember "the truth" on her own like in therapy. The third and largest group of people could not have cared less.

Then there was her quirky father. Bud had a stash of family photos he kept in a wooden box under the pool table. Mollie knew he perused these often. One day he told Mollie that he would like to pass these on to her. Mollie was honored.

A year after this Mollie asked to see the photos.

Bud acted puzzled. "I don't know what you are talking about." He denied the existence of any photos or box.

Mollie knew this was odd and terribly wrong.

Finally Bud came up with some pictures. They had been shredded with scissors. This made no sense. Welcome to Mollie's life.

Helen was Mollie's rock most of the time. She was there to encourage Mollie. When Mollie was in the fourth grade, she struggled to learn how to play the flute. She ended up crying as she tried to toot her flute. Helen intervened.

"You have to play the flute or cry. You can't do both at the same time."

Yet, there were some instances where even Helen snapped. One night for no reason she became infuriated and chased Mollie throughout the house. Bud finally told Helen to stop. That's when Mollie vowed to herself to move out.

Mollie was around so many strange people with agendas that her everyday experience with the world was so off the beaten path that it could not be paved over fast enough.

Mollie was not sure about people's motives when they said and did odd things. Mollie maintained that she had more than her fair share of these weird encounters.

Another oddity happened when she moved into her St. Petersburg apartment. Her apartment complex was near MacDill Air Force Base in Tampa. Her neighbor was a divorced, rugged guy who stopped by and introduced himself as Mollie was waxing her car.

Chip introduced himself as a member of the CIA. He showed proof. It was a shiny, black plastic card that was the size of a credit card. The card listed his name and all of his awards like The Purple Heart. This array of honors was listed in raised, gold embossed print with the CIA eagle spread at the top. Mollie was impressed, but didn't know why he divulged this to her on their first meeting.

One day she ran into him on the steps. It was during the first Gulf War in Iraq's Operation Desert Storm. Chip was dressed in a brown suit that you could bounce quarters off of and then they would snap to attention. His glossy shoes could serve as mirrors. He was holding an attache case for his attache work. Chip informed Mollie that he was on his way to Iraq to hand deliver the huge amount of money agreed upon as a payout to Saddam Hussein after Operation Desert Storm.

Mollie believed him. She knew that no one would believe her.

Chip related the story to Mollie about how during Operation Desert Storm that the U.S. had Saddam Hussein at point blank gun range. When a soldier was given the order to shoot Hussein dead, the soldier wouldn't do it. The commanding officer ripped the soldier's stripes right off of his uniform. The implications affected history.

Clinton was elected President. Mollie went down to her car one Sunday morning to go to church. Chip drove up beside her in the parking lot. He told her that the President had ordered military jets to attack Bosnia. They were on their way as they spoke.

When Mollie returned from church, she turned on the TV. Clinton was holding a press conference. He said that he had ordered a strike on Bosnia earlier in the day, but changed his mind and ordered the jets to turn back. This was the first that the public had been informed about it.

There was no doubt in Mollie's mind. Chip was the real deal.

Because of others doubting her sanity for so very long, Mollie frequently bought into other's test of reality instead of hers. This plays havoc with self-esteem. Mollie's private belief system was much stronger than her public belief system. Did this mean that she was delusional? Why weren't others who were doing and saying strange things considered delusional?

Mollie's truth was that reality testing wasn't in black and white nor was it true or false.

Mollie had another instance where her reality testing was shaken and shaky. Her best friend at the time was originally from East Germany. Hilda's stepfather was a member of the SS during World War II. She said that Hitler had a double. Hilda's husband speculated that Hitler wasn't killed during World War II, but had escaped to South America where he lived until the mid-seventies. Mollie made a mental note to herself that her grandfather died in 1974.

Mollie mentioned to Hilda one time that her husband could well be in the CIA. Hilda denied it. Mollie held onto this belief after her Thanksgiving there.

Thanksgiving dinner is a celebration that does not need to turn into a cornucopia of consternation. That is what happened. Mollie was as helpless as the turkey lying in state in the middle of the dining room table. A wishbone could not have gotten Mollie out of this situation.

It started when Hilda called to issue Mollie's yearly invitation. Like always it was her ordinary two day before Turkey Thursday call before her culinary storm. Hilda's kitchen rained out rolls and muffins with a turkey tornado with humid moistness along with a cumulus cloud which hailed out cranberry stuffing and pounded out a sleet of pies.

After the phone rang, Mollie's mouth watered. Mollie welcomed Hilda's words as she described the small family gathering it would be. She said her mother-in-law, an elderly aunt, her husband, her eighteen year old son, herself, and Mollie would be there.

It was a small clan, but everyone was certainly capable of eating. They were all acquainted and equipped to engage in their yearly small talk. The talk wasn't that tiny, but it drew the line at any mention of aches and pains.

Thanksgiving Day is one of those days where a turkey is glad to be breathing. Since it wasn't raining, there was no chance that a turkey would stare into the sky and drown itself. Other turkeys didn't have any choice about ending up on dinner tables. It goes to show that every turkey trots to a different drumstick.

Driving to Hilda's house Mollie gave herself the latitude of gratitude as she counted her blessings. Thanksgiving needs to count.

The only other cars on the road were filled with people on the way to potential heartburn. Football, food, families, and friends. It didn't get much better than this.

The slope up to Hilda's home curved around until Mollie reached their driveway. From the front there was no clue of a pool in back with a waterway behind that. Boats were moored there. It was essential to go boating at high tide and get back before low tide. There were several pairs of shoes permanently stuck in the muck from getting the boat in as the water had ebbed. The sucking pull of the muck almost pulled the socks off of some. This muck is a second cousin once removed from quicksand.

Mollie wheeled her car behind the Jaguar, Mercedes, and Porsche. Her car was not materialistically correct, but it could beat out other cars at lights.

The doorbell was carved out of ivory with a star sapphire backlit to invite a thumb to push it. Mollie felt her pleasant anticipation flow like gravy. She would be surrounded by a family she had known for years who were happy as yams. Her one glass of wine for the year would be poured with a flourish by the eighteen year old. Candles would flicker as people exhaled their conversation. The mood was comfort. Hilda's husband Dave would tell an anecdote with an amazing twist. The deciding dilemma was dessert with at least three calorie defying choices. The streusel was authentically German. The pumpkin pie had the whipped cream in a frenzy. The raspberry cheesecake demanded a fork.

Dave answered the door and gave Mollie two sincere kisses on each side of her glowing face. Hilda was not far behind with a hug and kisses. Mollie felt good. Yet, it reminded her of how starved she was for affection. When she read that people can barely subsist on six hugs a day, she felt sad. Mollie was lucky to be hugged six times in a year.

She was rarely touched and wondered why. An odd awareness quickly jolted through her. Where were the rest of the family members? There were strangers here. That explained the fancy cars in the driveway. The aromas were right. The company was not.

Introductions ran into each other. She recognized all but one couple. They were a North Korean woman and a New Zealand man. Another woman was there whom Mollie had met at one of Hilda's parties. All of a sudden for this occasion the woman had a New Zealand accent. Before she had a nondescript Midwestern voice. Her husband was an American with a shock of white hair. Hilda's son, mother-in-law, and Dave's elderly aunt were not there. Mollie had the urge to jump into her car and zoom to Dairy Queen.

Mollie sought refuge in the kitchen with Hilda. Even though Mollie's cooking skills were rudimentary, she could free muffins from tins, use potholders like a pro, and put butter in its place on the table. Hilda liked being in charge and used her East German genes to give orders.

Mollie followed them happily until everyone sat down to the fowl's finale.

The plentiful blessings in the form of food were passed around the table. Wine was poured for those who wanted to tempt any hint of alcoholism. The guests started a conversation with preliminary compliments about the food. It was impossible for Hilda to ruin anything when she cooked.

The airs in the dining room were clashing with the aromas. The North Korean woman was pretentiously pretentious. Her New Zealander boyfriend recounted a harrowing time he had on a yacht while battling a squall in The Gulf. Others were transfixed by his account, but Mollie was more intrigued when later in the dinner (during the second go-around of mashed potatoes) he mentioned that his arm almost got cut off in Syria. Everyone else told him that he should submit his squall story to Reader's Digest.

Mollie decided to enter into the conversation. She addressed the North Korean woman.

"What kind of sightseeing spots are there in North Korea?"

The North Korean woman answered with a careful nonchalance. "I don't know. I come downstairs in the morning and get into the limousine."

Mollie thought this was as odd as the whole dinner. She suspected that she was in the midst of CIA agents. All that was missing was Chip.

****

Mollie lived in St. Petersburg for five years. Then she moved to the Sarasota area because of her new job.

The beaches are beautiful in this section of Florida. The Chamber of Commerce isn't exaggerating its claims. Dolphins leap out of The Gulf as if posing for postcards. Beach goers dig their toes into the sand that is as powdery as sugar. Residents don't have to go anywhere for vacation. They have it all right there.

Mollie's stress accumulated. Her new psychiatrist wasn't very effective. Once he had her wait three hours until he saw her for her appointment.

Bud and Helen came to visit. They stayed overnight with Mollie. She was unraveling. Not only was she unraveling, but she was delusional She thought her parents physically assaulted her in her sleep. Mollie was psychiatrically hospitalized the next evening.

It was awful. Patients were screaming in the hallways all night long. Mollie was going without sleep which she desperately needed. She signed a legal document to release her from this emotional prison. Signing it meant she risked being committed against her will for a lengthy period of time. Her psychiatrist was young and always had hickeys on his neck when he arrived. He treated Mollie as if she were the enemy.

Mollie knew some of the staff from working with them years earlier at another Tampa psychiatric hospital. One day one of these nurses Mollie knew gave Mollie her medication. She looked at Mollie and said, "When is this going to end?"

Mollie didn't know what she was talking about. It was another one of those exasperating, inane comments.

One other peculiar incident happened while Mollie was hospitalized there. Mollie observed a patient in her seventies. She had egret white straight hair. On the day she was discharged she came over to Mollie.

She leaned over and spoke to Mollie. "I'm sorry I didn't have the chance to get to know you. I wish you the best."

Mollie peered into those intense azure eyes. Except for her hair the woman's profile was that of Bobby Kennedy. What a perfect cover that was to hide his whereabouts.

Mollie rescinded her legal document and was soon sprung from the hospital. Then she was able to rest. She concluded that psychiatrists detest having their authority challenged.

About a year passed, if that. Mollie began to hallucinate auditorily. She heard drums and chanting in the distance. The music she listened to in her car seemed to morph and be off key. The lyrics were different. Mollie was different.

Mollie went to the local general hospital because she was having chest pains. She was hooked up to a machine that bonged musical tones periodically. It felt as if the tones were going into her body. At nine o'clock at night she was released. She didn't understand the purpose of that treatment and no one explained the results.

She had taken a cab to the hospital and didn't have enough money to get home. She asked a police officer if he would give her a ride. He put her in the back seat of the car. Mollie told him that she did not want to go home. She didn't tell him that she thought her house was haunted. Mollie heard the policeman radio in, "I have a bitch without a collar." Mollie knew he was talking about her.

They ended up at a local psychiatric hospital where Mollie worked part-time. She requested to go there. They admitted her involuntarily.

The next morning Mollie vaguely recalled being encircled by psychiatric techs and nurses. She went up to certain ones and called them "zombies." Mollie was fading fast. She had not gone to the bathroom in twenty-four hours and again was operating on sleep deprivation.

WHOOSH! Urine poured out of her like a yellow waterfall. The standoff was over. The embarrassment was not.

Eventually Mollie was released from the hospital. Her supervisor at the hospital and the head of human resources met with her after she got out. They were not thrilled that Mollie had been a patient there.

"We tried to have you transferred to another hospital, but no one would take you."

Mollie was not sure whether or not to take this personally. They made her promise never to come back there as a patient.

Mollie worked a few more months there. She was mortified because at least one of the techs she urinated in front of worked with her. A patient who was hospitalized at the same time Mollie had been was in one of the groups Mollie led. A sense of shame enveloped Mollie like she had never experienced. She quit this part-time job.

Less than a year later Mollie began decompensating again. She stayed up all night battling what she believed were demons in her bedroom. They were small rings of light surrounding spots of darkness. Mollie extinguished them by taking aim with her eyes and blinking. They were dispersed one by one like this after hours on end of blinking.

The next morning she went to work at her job at an outpatient clinic. An ex-client came in and stood in the lobby as he told Mollie, "It isn't every day that you meet a superhero."

Mollie knew that he knew that she had defeated the demons.

By lunchtime there were men with walkie talkies swarming all over the building. Mollie wanted to hide because she thought this had something to do with her. A man with a camera on his shoulder like one used for remotes on TV came into her office and filmed the photographs on her bulletin board.

The next afternoon a coworker came into Mollie's office and plunked herself into a chair. Karen was known for her meltdown proclivity which Mollie had never witnessed. Mollie knew she had a good heart. Karen volunteered with helping retired racing greyhounds. Karen was passionate about these precious dogs. She was outraged about how the dogs were starved before a race and then punished if they lost a race.

Karen looked at Mollie with her Julia Robert's smile. "Don't you think this last week has been a miracle? It has been a miracle."

Mollie didn't know what she meant. Someone suddenly called Karen out of Mollie's office. Then another bizarre thing happened.

Mollie clearly heard the quick "cuckoo, cuckoo" of a cuckoo clock. Mollie didn't know whether this applied to her or to Karen or to both of them.

Mollie questioned whether she was auditorily hallucinating. She wondered what the "miracle" was that Karen was talking about. Did it have something to do with her? She was puzzled. To distract herself she turned on her computer and went to a jigsaw puzzle site to move some more puzzle pieces around.

The next day Mollie went into work more sleep deprived. In the afternoon she went to her colleague's office next to hers. She had the distinction of being that one person in the office in whom everyone confided. Diane and Mollie both were designated as the two people in the office addicted to Pepsi®. Diane was surfing the Internet when Mollie appeared at the door.

Mollie told her about the mysterious drawer in her desk. She would empty it and then it seemed to magically fill up again. Mollie told her how frustrating this was.

Mollie had not talked to Diane in months. Diane got Mollie up to speed about her life.

Then Diane made one of those oblique statements that had plagued Mollie all of her life. She told Mollie, "When this is over, you can go wherever you want."

Mollie thought a moment. "I've always wanted to meet the Kennedys. That's where I want to go."

When Mollie was writing this book, she realized what may have happened. Months before this she had entered an Oprah Winfrey contest to go on a cross-country trip with her. She had sent a tape into the show where her coworkers gave testimonials about why Mollie should be picked to win. Maybe she had won and the show was going to surprise her.

That would explain the camera filming in her office. That would explain the walkie talkies. Maybe it was a security detail for Oprah. Maybe that was the "miracle" that Karen referred to that day. Maybe that was why a coworker who had never watched Oprah just a couple of months previously now said she "hated" Oprah after Mollie returned from her hospitalization.

Maybe the show pulled the plug on Mollie's win because of stigma reasons. Mollie hoped not.

Mollie did not fulfill her wish to meet the Kennedys or "go wherever" she wanted. Instead, she went back into the hospital.

Just prior to this hospitalization Mollie decided she needed an exorcism. If she were related to Hitler and her father had something to do with Kennedy's assassination, then she wanted the evil within her expunged. She asked for Diane's help and it was arranged at Diane's Episcopal church. Mollie was so discombobulated that once she arrived at the church she got lost and the exorcism didn't happen. It was an exorcism in futility.

Mollie was assigned to a female Albanian psychiatrist nicknamed Dr. Terrific. Mollie and Dr. Terrific spent most of their sessions disagreeing with each other. Mollie finally had enough. She confronted Dr. Terrific.

"This isn't treatment. All you do is argue with me."

Dr. Terrific looked at her and did not disagree.

The psychiatric unit was full of yellers who spewed obscenities night and day. It was not a place for the sleep deprived.

Mollie had started writing a book about her life and hauled it everywhere with her on the unit. She latched onto it like it was her identity. It was.

Dr. Terrific released Mollie from the hospital after a short while. Mollie had her as her outpatient psychiatrist. She saw a Licensed Clinical Social Worker Turquoise Blue as her therapist.

Months later Mollie lost her job. It had nothing to do with her mental illness history, yet it probably didn't help matters. Mollie went on unemployment and on a long job hunt. She wasn't finding anything. There was that adage though.

"If at first you don't succeed, try center field..."

CHAPTER 19

Mollie eventually found another job. It was a part-time position with a hospice. There was an extensive orientation or training period. Mollie was assigned a preceptor whom she shadowed. Becky was a quiet, serious type who seemed to have been blunted by all the death she had been around. She was absolutely expressionless.

The second week of this orientation was the first for Mollie to accompany Becky to a condo where the husband of a woman had just died. The funeral home attendant wheeled the body out while Becky and Mollie were there comforting the widow. The widow asked about how to close her husband's mouth which hung open after his death. Mollie felt like crying. She managed to keep it together.

As they were leaving, the widow saw them to the door. Her parting words were, "I don't know why anyone would want to do the work you do."

Mollie wasn't sure she knew why either.

A couple of times Becky pointed out Dr. Richards who was the hospice's physician. Mollie got a good look at him.

A month later things began to unravel and so did Mollie. She went to a staff meeting where it was announced, "No one is to say anything."

A guy walked in who was introduced as Dr. Richards. It wasn't Dr. Richards. The Dr. Richards whom Mollie had seen had gray hair, was close to sixty years old, and wore glasses. This fake Dr. Richards was in his thirties with peroxide blonde hair. Mollie wasn't sure what was going on. It bothered her.

Dr. Richards led the meeting in a flip way. It was decided that Mollie and a nurse would meet him in some patients' homes.

As they were driving away from their final visit, the nurse acted like she were talking sotto voce into a microphone tucked into her shirt. She said, "He will be leaving by helicopter." A little later she did the same thing, but said, "She realizes things have to change."

Mollie was glad when the day was over and she did not have to shadow this nurse anymore.

Mollie was back with her preceptor. That turned weird too. She asked Mollie if she had ever been to Hawaii.

"No, but I've always wanted to go there."

The preceptor didn't blink. "You might want to go there now."

What did that mean? It was another thing that didn't make sense to Mollie.

Once again Mollie began to decompensate. She did not sleep. She got a call from the hospice. "Don't come in again until we call you." There was no explanation.

This was too much stress for Mollie. She could not afford to lose another job. She could not afford to go crazy again either.

She did.

Mollie got into her car. She had the premonition that her town was going to be bombed so she was going to drive as far as she could to escape that. The air had a dusty, dry clay quality to it. Mollie believed this meant that places nearby had already been bombed.

She ended up in Tampa and tried to go to the FBI, but they had moved from the building where they had been previously located. Mollie had the belief that her FBI

Agent brother was there. He had talked to her on the phone recently and asked, "Have you received a rather sizable check in the mail? You will." Mollie hadn't and didn't.

From there Mollie drove north and pulled off the road. She called her parents. Her father announced with discovery in his voice, "Mollie, you're sick!" Helen got on the phone and asked Mollie where she was.

"I'm on my way to Ocala. I want to be safe."

"The safest place you can be is at home."

Mollie turned around to head home. She decided to try a new way back. She got lost. As she struggled to get her bearings, she came across a church in a woodsy setting. Mollie decided to stop in. She entered the side door and was thrust in the middle of a church women's lunch. It was the type of lunch where people stood around with paper plates. Mollie asked one woman if she could speak to the priest.

Father Bill emerged from the group and was polishing the last bit of food from his plate. He invited Mollie back to his study.

He made a strange comment. "You are a rich woman."

Mollie wondered whether there was any end to the odd stuff that people said to her

Father Bill repeated his statement. "You are a rich woman." Then he suggested that Mollie get a baseball bat to put beside her bed.

He asked what Mollie wanted to talk about. For some reason Mollie asked about the Rapture.

Mollie learned from Father Bill that this wasn't part of Catholicism belief. They talked some more. Father Bill said he would like her to attend church there.

Mollie would have liked to do that, but had no idea how she got there. She wasn't even sure how to get home.

After a few wrong turns Mollie found her way home. It had been a long day. Another unanswered question was added to her mental list. Was she a rich woman? Her bank account's answer to that was, "No."

Mollie began to have uncomfortable physical sensations. She felt like she were being electrically shocked and at other times she felt as if she were being shot. The pain was intense.

She began being paranoid of her next door neighbor who was a short, swarthy, and menacing guy. After she returned home, he shot off what sounded like three missiles. The sound of them being launched was a thousand times louder than bottle rockets. Mollie had a suspicion for a while that he was digging a tunnel underneath her house to harbor fugitives.

It was another sleepless night for Mollie. After midnight she was walking across her living room floor when she heard her father's voice. It boomed. "You are going to hell."

By the next morning Mollie had more auditory hallucinations. She was hearing a continuous loop of "Mary Had a Little Lamb" and church choir music.

She called the hospice because she hadn't heard from them about when they wanted her to return. Without any explanation Mollie was fired.

Mollie totally unraveled. She was hospitalized again under the care of Dr. Terrific. When she got to the hospital, she saw the newspaper headlines. Three missiles had hit Jordan...

Then Mollie began smelling apple pies baking as well as smelling pot roast. Later Dr. Terrific explained how this could be attributed to Temporal Lobe Epilepsy or TLE. TLE can go along with bipolar illness. Mollie was put on anti-seizure medication. Just prior to this hospitalization Mollie drove to St. Petersburg to see her therapist Turquoise Blue. As she drove there, she had a headache that felt like her two brain lobes were being split apart. Perhaps this was due to the TLE too.

It wasn't too long until Mollie was released from the hospital. She felt like her mind was impaired. She couldn't always think of the words she wanted to say. This was the heaviest that she had ever been medicated.

Mollie followed up with Turquoise Blue and Dr. Terrific. Mollie told Turquoise of all of the strange, inexplicable things that had happened to her over her lifetime. Turquoise suggested that Mollie create a timeline of all of these things. Mollie did so. Turquoise acknowledged that she had never come across any client with so many of these oddities. Mollie was heartened to be validated this way. Turquoise brought up the point that maybe people "were messing" with her head. Why would so many want to do that?

Mollie also liked Turquoise because she was down to earth. She had a Tickle Me Elmo in her office that made Mollie laugh like she hadn't for a long time.

What didn't make her laugh was that Mollie found out that Dr. Terrific had lived in Boston for many years. There was the possible Kennedy connection again.

Mollie told Dr. Terrific about the novel she was writing. She brought up how she was afraid she would offend people with what she wrote.

Dr. Terrific reacted with anger. "SCREW THE PRICKS!"

This type of permission helped fuel Mollie to finish this book.

First, Bud had one more surprise up his sleeve. Mollie was talking to him on the phone when he asked her, "Have you ever read <u>Mein Kampf</u>?"

"No."

"Well, I'm looking at it on the bookshelf in front of me. Would you like to read it?"

"Yes, I would."

Several months later Bud told her that he didn't have the book. "I lied."

As a fortune cookie said that Mollie got one time, "Three things cannot be long hidden: the sun, the moon, and the truth."

EPILOGUE

This book is based on a true story which is mine. All of the actions and interactions involving me directly are true.

However, I don't believe I am related to Hitler now. My self-esteem must have improved with my medication effectively kicking in.

By writing this book I wanted to show how reality and delusions are difficult to tell apart. Many things have not made sense in my life. Was the black walnut from LBJ's ranch and my father's company using The Texas Book Depository coincidental? What about all of the inane things people said to me? These things complicate reality testing. It is said that in paranoia there is always a grain of truth. See how things are mixed up?

What is the truth here? There are many things to wonder about that happened to me. I can't explain them all away as to being because of my bipolar illness.

This book is to make you pause and think. Maybe I wasn't completely delusional. You get a flavor of what I've been through and why. If nothing else you can see why madness is so maddening.

I believe who I am is still intact. I have not let anyone take away who I am.

Another purpose of this book is to show that even though a person suffers from mental illness, there can be lengthy times of remission. As my primary physician put it, "Bipolar people take medication and run around like the rest of us."

I apologize to my family for any pain that this portrayal may cause them. They have been truly supportive

of me and my struggle. I could not exist without their love.
Thank you.

February 28, 2009

.

THE TITLE

You may wonder about the title of this book
<u>Flamingos Can't Tap Dance</u>. A flamingo represents bipolar
disorder. It is an odd bird and it stands out. It is not
ordinary. A flamingo has two legs, but usually has one leg
that it stands on. It can't tap dance. That is a source of
frustration like the limitations imposed on a person who has
Bipolar Disorder.

Yet, there is an elegance to a flamingo and someone
with Bipolar Disorder can have this quiet dignity too.
When one has limitations, one must wing it. A flamingo
may not be able to tap dance, but it can strut. Someone
with Bipolar Disorder can hold their head up high too. Not
being able to tap dance or having Bipolar Disorder don't
need to be stigmas.

mollieann52@yahoo.com

www.ingramcontent.com/pod-product-compliance
Lightning Source LLC
Chambersburg PA
CBHW062142280526
45788CB00001B/266